TWAYNE'S WORLD AUTHORS SERIES (TWAS)

The purpose of TWAS is to survey the major writers —novelists, dramatists, historians, poets, philosophers, and critics—of the nations of the world. Among the national literatures covered are those of Australia, Canada, China, Eastern Europe, France, Germany, Greece, India, Italy, Japan, Latin America, the Netherlands, New Zealand, Poland, Russia, Scandinavia, Spain, and the African nations, as well as Hebrew, Yiddish, and Latin Classical literatures. This survey is complemented by Twayne's United States Authors Series and English Authors Series.

The intent of each volume in these series is to present a critical-analytical study of the works of the writer; to include biographical and historical material that may be necessary for understanding, appreciation, and critical appraisal of the writer; and to present all material in clear, concise English—but not to vitiate the scholarly content of the work by doing so.

Shen Ts'ung-wen

By HUA-LING NIEH
University of Iowa

Twayne Publishers, Inc.   ::   New York

895.13
SS46N

WITH THE ASSISTANCE OF WAN KIN-LAU

Acknowledgments

Warmest thanks are due the Chinese poet from Hong Kong, Wan Kin-lau, for his admirable research and for the initial translation of materials into English. He was especially helpful in the biographical portions of the book. The interest and devotion he gave the book added invaluable insight.

The Filipino novelist, Wilfredo Nolledo, has helped shape the biographical sections. I am also indebted for his assistance with the English text.

I am grateful to Elliott Anderson, from The Program in Creative Writing, for his help with the final English version, and to William Golightly for reading proof.

Professor John Gerber, Director of the School of Letters, was at all times sympathetic and encouraging. The Graduate College and Dean Spriestersbach have supported the writing of this book.

Mrs. Linda Tsou, East Asia Collection, Hoover Institute, Stanford University, was generous with books. Professor C. T. Hsia, Columbia University, kindly let me use some of the books necessary in the preparation of this work.

For permission to quote, acknowledgment is made to the following:

> Harvard University Press (Cambridge, 1960): *The May Fourth Movement* by Chow Tse-tsung.
> Thames and Hudson (London, 1961): *The Chinese Revolution* by Tibor Mende.
> Harvard University Press (Cambridge, 1966): *China's Response to the West* by Teng Ssu-yu and J. K. Fairbank.
> George Allen and Unwin, Ltd. (London, 1947): *The Chinese Earth* by Ching Ti and Robert Payne.

The International Writing Program offered both a congenial environment to the foreign writer, and many practical aids.

Because of the University of Iowa's unique hospitality to the creative writer, from whatever country, I have been able to

85480

complete this critical-biographical study of a Chinese fiction writer, while at the same time continuing to write and publish my own fiction. Thanks also go to The Louis W. and Maud Hill Family Foundation of St. Paul for its help and its interest in translation.

Contents

Preface

When Lu Hsün, one of China's literary giants, died in 1936, an unofficial ritual of continuity was performed. Some of the Chinese reading public believed that the void left by the grand master could be filled by Shen Ts'ung-wen. At first, Shen Ts'ung-wen seemed an unlikely heir to the throne of sociological literature. For one thing, the younger Shen had nothing in common with the older writer. As artists, they were as different as rice and corn. There was a toughness, an inexorable quality of pessimism to the essential Lu Hsün which invariably colored his work. He was the unforgiving observer of everything that was ludicrous and decadent in Chinese society, most notably during the period of China's civil wars. Nor was domestic lunacy his only concern. The encroachment of Western industrialization, Lu Hsün feared, might wreak further havoc on his ill-prepared countrymen. With this vision, the angry author had no alternative but to portray his people as dupes and pawns, as species of sick men. Like a disenchanted doctor, he pinpointed sores, opened old wounds, without once looking beyond his patient, and wasting few words on landscape or sunset.

But contrasting life styles are never grounds for contesting a succession, literary or otherwise. For his part, Shen Ts'ung-wen took upon himself the role of "recorder." Whereas Lu Hsün's work source had been the town, Shen's became the country. Nothing if not flexible, Shen grew from adolescence to manhood precariously balanced between national political hysteria and repression. Intermittent periods of military service exposed him to life in rural hamlets and their attendant horrors. It is to his credit that these less pleasant experiences did not undermine his appreciation of the inherent beauty of country life, and of the virtues of country men and peasants he was to celebrate. Even the barbarous warlords could not diffuse Shen's abiding faith in people in whose innate goodness he saw the structural framework of a more responsive country.

Shen Ts'ung-wen's literary concerns, logically enough, nourished themselves on the legacy of all great artists. As a modern writer, he inherited and benefited from the Chinese literary heritage. His various wanderings provided him with an eye for color and detail; his appetite for books gave him foundations on which he built his own monuments. As for Western industrial influence, Shen believed that any such invasion could not seriously affect the life force of China. Whereas Lu Hsün expressed his despair and self-criticism in bitter satire which he founded in hatred and held up to the public like so many critical mirrors, Shen chose subjects and a prose style that were infinitely more subdued, even delicate. As a survivor of several bloodbaths and ideological upheavals, Shen Ts'ung-wen became a writer who waded through mankind's misery to get to its basic humanity. He wrote with classic simplicity, struggling to match the right words to his noble passions. A reappraisal of his early fiction may somewhat dim the luster of the eminent position he occupies in Chinese letters today, because his early prose was often flawed. However, his later stories compensate for their imperfections and excesses by presenting men, women, and children as they were in China—and as they will always be. Invariably, his fictional characters are as credible as the seasons they endure, the hunger they suffer, the children they bear. This lyrical and graphic portrait of Chinese life is Shen Ts'ung-wen's contribution to literature; and it is this which places him at the forefront of modern Chinese fiction writers.

Of all Chinese writers in the thirties, Shen Ts'ung-wen was one of the most widely read and important, but is now, on mainland China, one of the most silent, devoting himself not to fiction writing, but to the study of porcelains, silk design, and bronze mirrors of the T'ang and Sung dynasties. As a true artist, Shen Ts'ung-wen is a typical and tragic example of the fate that has befallen most writers in modern China, perhaps in the modern world, who have tried to keep their artistic integrity. He was dismissed by the leftists in the thirties as empty and thoughtless because he showed no interest in the dialectics of the left. Ironically, however, his critical views of the social conditions of his time inhibited his acceptance by the ruling government (then, the Nationalist party), which

Preface

meant that some of his works were censored. Critics, even when they have appraised him from the point of view of aesthetics, have done no more than measure him as a "stylist" or an "impressionist." Few critics have tried to understand him as a modern fiction writer. This criticism of Shen Ts'ung-wen's work will focus on his modern themes, style, and imagery. Since his works are not so well known to Western readers as are the works of Western writers, I will devote several chapters to the significant aspects of Shen's life and his time before I analyze his works as modern literature. I hope this book will help the Western reader understand a modern Chinese master, and offer insight into the plight and problems of the imaginative individual artist trapped between hostile ideologies.

HUA-LING NIEH

University of Iowa
Iowa City, Iowa.

Chronology

1903   Born in Phoenix Town, West Hunan, on the River Yüan.

1915   Entered Primary School in Phoenix Town.

1917   Entered Preparatory Military School in September.

1918   Left Phoenix Town as an army private for Yüan-ling (also called Ch'en-chou).

1920   Worked in Yüan-chou as a revenue collector.

1922   Spring in West Hunan; winter, traveled to Peking.

1923   Began to contribute prose to newspapers under the pseudonym Hsiu Yün-yün. Met Hu Yeh-p'in and Ting Ling.

1925   Worked as dispatcher and proofreader for *Modern Critic* and made his first appearance in the journal *Yü-szu,* June 29, with publication of a short story.

1926   November, Pei-hsin Press (New North Press) published his first book, *The Ducks.*

1928   Shen, Hu Yeh-p'in, and Ting Ling edited *Jen-chien Yüeh-k'an* (*The Human World Monthly*), and *Hung-hei Yüeh-k'an* (*The Red and Black Monthly*).

1929   After *The Red and Black Monthly* folded for financial reasons, began teaching in the Wu-sung Chinese Institute.

1930   In Peking, then teaching at the University of Wuhan, Wu-ch'ang, Hupeh.

1931   Father died. Hu Yeh-p'in arrested on January 17; executed in February. Shen returned to Peking.

1933   Taught at Tsingtao University and on September 9 married an ex-student, Chang Chao-ho.

1934   October, in Peking as editor of the literary page of *Ta-kung Pao.* Ting Ling arrested. First son, Lung-lung born to Shen and Chang.

1935   Winter in Peking. Began revision of the thirty-five volumes of his published work.

1936   In Peking. Winter, Lu Hsün died in Shanghai. April, *The Selected Works of Shen Ts'ung-wen* published by Wan-hsiang Press.

1937   In Peking. June, a second son, Hu-hu, born. Returned to West Hunan.

1938 In Kunming, teaching at Southwest Associated University.
1940 In Kunming. April, became editor of the magazine *Chan-kuo ts'e*.
1942 In Kunming. Wrote the preface to *The Long River*, a novel, criticizing censorship.
1945 In Kunming. War of resistance against the Japanese ended with Japan's surrender August 14.
1946 Resumed teaching in Peking University in the autumn.
1948 In Peking. Attacked by propaganda posters for being a "Writer of Empty-headedness."
1950 In T'sing-hua Yüan. Tried to commit suicide but failed. Autumn, forced to enroll in the People's Revolution University.
1951 Dismissed from Peking University. Sent to labels department in Peking Museum.
1956 Self-critical speech of self-revelation published February 8, in the *Kwang-ming Daily News*.
1957 In Peking. Nonfiction, *Designs in Chinese Silk and Linen* published by the Chinese Classical Art Press.
1958 *Bronze Mirrors in the T'ang and Sung Dynasties* published by the Chinese Classical Art Press.
1961 Toured Ching-kang Shan, Kiangsi, with the Chinese Writers Association. Poems and essays inspired by the trip appeared in *People's Literature*, Peking.
1963 Essays on Chinese festivals appeared in the March issue of *People's Literature*, Peking.

Hereafter, no documented evidence of Shen Ts'ung-wen's life.

CHAPTER 1

From the River Yüan: One More Tributary

PART of the Chinese soul may be glimpsed in the birthplace of Shen Ts'ung-wen. Consider West Hunan, where arteries of the Yangtse River flow through mountains dotted with caves, where land and inhabitant complement each other: the highways are nearly impassable, and farm soil is poor. Miao[1] tribespeople who inhabit the area dabble in exorcism. Removed from the pressures of urban life, the scene suggests a Chinese scroll painting, at once placid and tribal. The River Yüan teems with rowboats and schooners, oil boats, Ch'en brook boats, and Mayang boats[2] and mastless boats. Wuling is the legendary fisherman's home. Here, T'ao-yüan, the "Peach Flower Spring" of the poet T'ao Yüan-ming, is found. West Hunan is also rich in folklore. Then, as now, according to tradition, ancestors of the Ch'in dynasty are abroad. On the road to Ch'en-chou, fabled for its magical charm, the eye may recoil at a bizarre scene: mummy drivers herding their rows of corpses across the highway. Perhaps the crudities of geography, the nuances of mysticism, can sometimes forge the vital components of a creative spirit. In Shen Ts'ung-wen's case, these elements certainly contributed to the making of one of China's leading literary figures.

Shen Ts'ung-wen was born in 1903 in the village of Feng-huang (Phoenix Town, Hunan) on a tributary of the River Yüan, near the borders of Kweichow and Szechwan. Steeped in military tradition, the family boasted of a general (Shen's grandfather) in Kweichow who had died of battle wounds. Several uncles were also in the army, and Shen's father had rendered service as a sort of bodyguard to the commander of the Taku forts, Tientsin. Before her death, Shen's grandmother expressed the hope that there would be another general in the clan.

From the beginning, Shen found school a nuisance, something

15

he tried to avoid whenever he could. The teachers who determined to harness his energies and redirect his mind he ignored
with dexterity and contempt. Brooks were more interesting than
books; classrooms were to be avoided like the plague. Nature
beckoned, and nothing seemed more natural than running free
in the woods or wading in the river. Neither official reprimand
nor paternal discipline could wean him from the out-of-doors.
Once, his father even threatened to cut off one of his fingers if
he did not change his ways. If Shen was frightened by the threat,
he was frightened even more by the notion of having to surrender
his natural playground. To save his finger, he promised to behave,
but then he fled to his first love—the fields, the windswept fields,
which even at that early age were teaching him the language
of a future craft.

A soldier until his middle age, the elder Shen looked to his son
to carry on a military tradition. If the family name were to be
inscribed on future monuments—if the clan were to be honored by
future feats of glory—then the young Shen would have to follow
his father's example.

Such ambitions, however, did not interest the boy. He was
more interested in following the lead of an older cousin who took
it upon himself to educate Shen, not according to books and
military discipline, but to fresher vistas of adventure. Nothing
seemed sweeter than the freedom of juvenilia, and fabrication
became an art. Soon, Shen was an accomplished, almost patho-
logical liar. A nearby river had become so inviting that he and his
companions would splash in it for half a day, almost driving their
tutor out of his wits. Swimming was no longer a sport, but
something of an obsession. Of this early experience, Shen was
later to write: "That my emotion flows with ease, remains unstale,
is largely due to the influence of water. The more beautiful part
of my childhood is inseparable from water. Such was my school-
ing. . . . Whatever sense and sensibility I have was purified by
water. . . ."[3]

Primary school did nothing to change the boy's attitude. Rather
than go to school, he wandered through the suburbs and out of
town into the mountains. In school, he had been taught to
worship textbooks and blackboards; but what faded text could
compare to the rhythms and the variety of street scenes? As he

wandered through town, the variety of faces and occupations
fascinated him. In the temples, people wove rope and bamboo
mats, manufactured incense. Elsewhere, they toiled at more
menial chores and with more menial hopes: they chattered, they
quarreled, they laughed and sang. Without realizing it, Shen
the dropout had slowly, laboriously, begun his apprenticeship
as a writer.

Self-indulgence had a price, of course. At school, the truant
was made to sit before a portrait-altar of Confucius and was
spanked until he showed some remorse. The venerable old man
of China seemed to look on sadly. The punishment varied and
sometimes Shen was made to kneel on the floor to wait out the
burning of a candle. The boy seemed to endure the wrath of centuries and the stiffness in his body by thinking of the ponds he
had been swimming in, of the ripening fruits on the trees he had
yet to climb, of the mountains he longed to explore. At home,
he had to suffer his parents' anger meekly.

Thinking that their son's truancy was somehow the result of his
teacher's permissiveness, the family transferred the boy to a new
school farther away from home. Such a step, unfortunately,
merely increased Shen's wanderlust. En route to his new school,
he was again diverted by several places of interest: a needleshop
where an old man with overlarge eyeglasses, head bowed, whet-
ted needles; an umbrella factory whose open door revealed to
pedestrians several apprentices bent to their labors; a leather
bootshop with its pot-bellied bootmaker baring his round, hairy
belly as he worked on his leather goods; a barber shop, open
day and night, wherein a customer clutching a small wooden
tray sat awkwardly while his hair was cut; a dye factory whose
numerous, sturdy Miaos trod an elevated, indented stone mill,
swaying left and right, right and left. There were three beancurd
shops run by the Miaos whose turbaned, slim-waisted women
crooned sweetly to their young strapped to their backs like so
many Indian papooses, or amused them with bright brass ladles.
And there was a mill that produced cornstarch, where donkeys
tugged endlessly at a revolving mortar. On the roofs of shacks
white noodles were left to dry in the sun; a butcher's table offered
quivering fresh pork; a paper shop sold scrolls of offerings for
the dead; another displayed sedan chairs for hire to newlyweds,

and tinctured pictures of blue-faced devils, fish dragons, golden lads, and jade lasses. Each day there were fewer conjugal chairs and more paper offerings. Business flourished. As if immune to fortune, the shopkeepers continued to work as impassively as ever, gilding, powdering, and coloring their goods.

As colorful as these outlying districts were, nothing impressed Shen as much as the prison situated west of town. Early in the morning, grim men, manacled hand and foot, would pour out of the prison on their way to hard labor at the Yamen. In the execution square, dogs tore at decapitated bodies. Some strange compulsion made Shen pick up a pebble or rock to hurl at those rotting bodies. Sometimes he would even poke at a cadaver with a stick to see if it could still move. More often, however, he gathered stones in his satchel to throw at the dogs.

Southside, on the river bank, oxen were slaughtered. For hours on end, Shen would watch the grisly show as men struck down beast after beast. So precise and balletlike were the killings that in time Shen knew everything, down to the last detail, there was to know about the bloody business. Farther along, on a narrow street, old men could be found cutting bamboo husk while two boys squatted on the ground, weaving mats. Nearby was a smithshop whose interior was dominated by a smelting furnace. Here, a boy could be found working the bellows, pulling determinedly with both hands, his body dropped forward and swaying backward, eliciting from that monstrous contraption a ferocious roar.

When the river was in flood, a barefoot Shen waded the puddles. Occasionally, the current carried logs, pieces of furniture, pumpkins, odds and ends. From the bridge, young men dangling by a length of rope would lower themselves into the water to salvage whatever caught their fancy below.

These formative years were rich, many-colored, and violent. And Shen, the truant, would not forget a single drop of butcher's blood, not a hair from a decapitated head, not a noodle, not a scrap of tin, not a strand of hemp, not one bead of perspiration, not even the glimmer from the blacksmith's anvil. Each experience would become a layer of his skin, part of his vital currency, which like a miser, he would hoard—every coin, scrap, and trinket. Shen was later to rely on this wealth in an article, *My Writing and the Waters*:

After fifteen years, there is an inseparable relationship between my life and the River Ch'en by which I lived for five years. Not a day passed but that I did not have contact with my river. I used to spend the night on bridges and dredge ferries, so that whatever is memorably sad or happy is for me always soaking wet. . . .

Even though I left my home on the river bank, most of the stories I have written are about the river. The settings of the stories I like best are river and shipboard stories. The characters in my works come from ships and river banks. The gloomy atmosphere in my writing issues from dark rainy days of the south I remember. If there is anything noteworthy in my style, it is because I remember the dialects of the people who live on the water.[4]

But Shen did not wander idly. He learned and he began to question: Why should the eyes of donkeys be covered when they are pushing stone mills? Why should a rapier be dipped in water for temper after it has been fired? Why should the sculptor of Buddha figures carve wood into human shapes and then gild it with sheets of gold so thin as to be nearly incredible? How could a cobbler bore such a round hole in a bronze plate and engrave such delicately wrought flowers round it?

. . . . Watching, listening, smelling dead snakes and rotting straw, the body-odor of butchers, and then the scent rising from the kilns after rain. I could not then describe these sensations in words, but could detect them instantly. The squeak of a bat, the sigh of a throat, the rattle of yellow striped snakes hidden in fields and caves, the faint sounds fish make in the dark—because these sounds were registered for me by their uniqueness, and even now I can recall them distinctly. . . .[5]

CHAPTER 2

And the River Turns Red

VIOLENCE had long been an accepted part of life in the
Shen family. All young Shen's cousins were in the army; it
was no secret that the Republican Revolution of 1911 in West
Hunan was kindled by Shen's father and uncles. The following
passages from Shen Ts'ung-wen's *Autobiography* recount in detail
the exciting moments of one revolution he experienced:

I was glad to hear my father say I could stay in town with him. I
remember clearly the next evening the particularly interesting scene
of my uncle, red in the face, whetting his cutlass in the lamplight.
I watched for a while and then I went to my father's study, to
watch him clean his shotgun. Since a lot of the folks had left, the
house seemed much bigger. I used to be afraid but I was not afraid
at all that day. I wasn't sure what, but I knew something new and
important was about to happen. I listened to my father and the
others talking. They were usually calm, but now seemed quite agitated. They stammered when they talked. They rubbed the guns
and smiled at each other for reasons I didn't know. But, I smiled
as they smiled.

I saw them work in the sunlight, and saw them consult each
other under the lamplight. My tall uncle would run out the door
for a while and run back in to talk quietly. I pretended not to
notice, but counted how many times he ran out the door. That day,
he ran out nine times. The last time, I followed him out on the porch.
I said: "Uncle, why are you preparing to fight?"

"Hey, you, boy," he replied, "Go to bed, or cats will eat you. . . ."

I have no idea what happened outside and inside the town that
night. When I woke up the next morning, everyone in the family
had a white face and was whispering quietly. I was asked if I had
heard anything in the night. I shook my head no. There were people
missing from the house, it seemed. I counted and discovered
some uncles missing. The only man in the room was my father who
was sitting in his easy chair, his head down. He was silent. I remembered the preparations that had been made for the fight, and asked
him, "Papa, Papa, did you fight?"

20

"You boy," he said. "Don't babble. We were defeated last night. We lost all our men; several thousand were killed."

As we were talking, Tall Uncle returned with perspiration on his forehead, stammering—the Yamen had received four hundred and eleven trophy heads, a long string of ears, seven battle ladders, some cutlasses, and other things. More people had been killed across the river. Seven houses had been burned. No one was allowed to go onto the ramparts to see the damage.

When my father heard that four hundred heads had been taken, he said to Uncle, "Go see if little Han's is among them. Hurry up, hurry up."

Little Han was my dark, plump cousin. When I understood that he also had fought outside the city last night, I was worried. Hearing about so many heads and the string of ears outside the Yamen, I remembered the stories my father used to tell about killing the long hair bandits, and I felt delighted and frightened at the same time. I didn't know what to do. After washing my face, I went out to look at the sky which was dark, as though it might rain, and everything was very dim. I had used to hear a cake-seller's voice from the end of the street, and other sounds made by hawkers, but it was particularly quiet that day, like New Year's day. I wanted to go out and see the heads that I had never touched. Soon my chance came. My tall fourth uncle ran back to tell my father that Little Han's head was not one of the four hundred. He said there were a lot of people at the Yamen; all shops on the streets had been ordered to reopen. Old Master Chang also went out to see what had happened. My father asked me, "Hi, boy, are you afraid of heads? If not, you can come with me."

"I'm not," I said, "I want to see the heads." So I saw a big heap of dirty, blood-stained heads on the ground in front of the Yamen. The arcade was covered with heads. The several battle ladders were made of new bamboo—(they used newly cut bamboo from the mountain and nailed wooden slats horizontally across the ladder poles). From the wooden slats hung many heads. I was amazed and did not understand why all these people had been killed; I didn't understand why all these people had had their heads cut off. Not long after, I discovered the string of ears, the string, so strange, which not many see in a lifetime. My uncle asked me, "Little thing, are you afraid?" I gave a good answer. I said, "No, I'm not." I had heard many stories of battles and killings which were always about "heads like mountains, blood flowing to become a river." When I went to the opera, I always heard "thousands of troops and horses, both sides fighting to the death." I had seen a wooden human head on a red tray in the opera in which Ch'in Ch'iung, a legendary hero, wept over his friend's head, but I had never seen a real human head severed in battle. Now, there were so many heads in such a big heap and everyone of them dripping blood, freshly cut from human necks. I was not afraid, but I didn't understand why these people would let soldiers behead them. I suspected there had been some mistake.

Why had they been beheaded? I had many doubts. When I returned home, I asked my father. His answer was "Revolution," which was not a satisfactory answer at all. At that time, I thought that my father was a great man and that he knew innumerable things about the world, and I was amazed that he didn't know what this was all about. Now, I begin to understand that such things have never been lacking in the world, but that no one can adequately answer a child's question. . . .

The revolution had failed, but the killing had just begun. The town guards, after having carefully arranged for their defenses, began to send soldiers to the villages to arrest the rebels. Those who were arrested were asked one or two questions and were taken outside the town to be beheaded. Formerly, executions had been performed outside West Gate. Now, since the rebellion had taken place at the North Gate, those to be executed were taken to the river bank near the North Gate. In the beginning, the guards killed about one hundred people a day. For the killing of fifty prisoners, there would be twenty soldiers to do the job, and about thirty prisoners left standing to watch and wait their turn. Sometimes, the guards didn't strip the prisoners of their clothing, or tie them with rope, but just herded them together onto the river bank. Sometimes, those waiting to be executed stood a little away and were mistaken by the soldiers for onlookers. The soldiers forgot about them and went away. Those killed mostly came from the country. They were confused; they didn't know what was going on, and some of them only began to understand when they reached the river bank and were ordered to kneel down. Then they began to cry and to run about in panic. The executioners had only to run forward to chop them down.

This stupid killing lasted for about one month, then gradually subsided. Perhaps because the weather was becoming severely cold, no one worried about the bodies decomposing. When there was no time to bury the corpses, they were left where they had fallen. Or, perhaps they were left as a warning to the public. There were always between four and five hundred corpses lying on the river bank. Soon, there were too many prisoners for the local guards to manage. It seemed all the prisoners from the Miao villages would have to be beheaded. The local officials, when they reported to the governor, would usually say the revolution had been planned by the Miao tribes. The local officials were required to destroy everyone found to be revolutionary. Many people were arrested; most were very simple-minded—not clever enough to plead innocent, but the executioners themselves seemed frightened by all the killing. Several powerful local gentry who had secretly conspired with people outside the city to revolt, but who had not been discovered by the officials, sent a petition to the governor to ask that limits be set on the killing, and that there be some selection: those who deserved execution should be killed, but the innocent should be released. Everyday, one or two hundred innocent farmers were arrested. The officials could not let them all go, nor did they want to kill all of them. The dilemma was soon solved by arranging a procedure for selection, the responsibility for which was assigned to the Heavenly King worshipped by the local people. The soldiers led the prisoners to the temple, to the main parlor where each was made to cast a pair of bamboo rods: one face up and one face down was regular, and the prisoner was released; both faces up meant (light) Yang fodder, and also meant release; both faces down meant (dark) Yin fodder, and that the prisoner was condemned to die. Life or death depended on the cast. Those who were to die went to the left; those who were to live went to the right. A man who had been given two chances of three to live remained silent when it was determined he had to die; he lowered his head and walked to the left.

At that time, I was free and could go out of doors by myself. Whenever I had the chance, I would climb the ramparts to see the beheadings across the river. Whenever the men were killed and I couldn't be present to see the cutlass strike, I would compete with other boys to see who had the best eyesight by trying to estimate the total number of bodies on the river bank, or I would follow the prisoners to watch them cast bamboo rods at the temple. We saw how the villagers closed their eyes and cast with vigor. Some dared not open their eyes even though they were supposed to be released by the cast. We also saw some who were to die but who perhaps still remembered their calves, piglets and lambs. They looked sad, as though dissatisfied with the decision of the Heavenly King.

When I began to know "life," that was what I knew.[1]

In 1914, a primary school was established according to a new education system in the area. Shen attended the school in 1915. By autumn of 1917, when he had enrolled in the fourth grade, a civil war was raging against Yüan Shih-k'ai.[2] In self-defense, Hunan's local government formed an official military corps and organized a training camp for soldiers. While the martial air that had descended upon the city augured none too well for its residents, it was something of a relief to Shen's mother who had by this time despaired of ever suppressing her son's worldly proclivities. She felt she could not commend him for knowing the names of woods, herbs, plants, birds. She had not raised him to be a potter, even though he had a knack for porcelain making. Nor did she want him to be a sculptor, even though he could cast statues. She thought that what her son needed most was discipline, and she sent him to one of the newly established military training camps. At first, the choice seemed perfect. Now a recruit, Shen went through the paces necessary to the training of a soldier. Perhaps in vindication of his family's wishes, the boy even applied for higher positions in the camp. While he never did attain the rank of a regular serviceman in the corps, he nevertheless passed all the requirements, weathered all the necessary drills.

The Hunan military team was disbanded in 1918 after the official trainer terminated his own office. Altogether, Shen had had eight months of intensive military training. The art of physical combat toughened his body; the regimentation of camp life contained his wayward tendencies. Back home, however, life had become difficult. His father was away from home again, an elder sister was dead, and a large portion of the family's property had been sold to pay off debts—this in addition to an initial loss suffered by the family when much of their treasure had been lost during the Boxer Uprising.[3] Instead of a warm homecoming, the trainee was met with ill-tidings, and the fact that now his mother was willing to send him out into the world.

On July 16, 1918, at the age of fifteen, Shen, with the rank of militiaman, left home for the garrison at Ch'en-chou (also called Yüan-ling), a city larger than Phoenix Town, and many miles away.

Eight years later, Shen was to recount his adventures in a

story "Leaving Home." Leaving home for the first time meant
hiking sixty miles to river transportation and from there traveling
another two days by boat to the garrison. He walked along trails,
peeking into shop windows, marking the wares: huge fibered
ropes, loads of hard wood, small fishing baskets, delicately
wrought knives, firepokers, mouthpieces for pipes. He would
squat over these articles "like a gentleman examining antiques."

Garrison life, as it turned out, was much like life in the training camp in Phoenix Town. For calisthenics, the troops performed a morning sprint—and no one ever knew whether this was
to groom him for chasing outlaws or to sharpen his reflexes
in the event that it was necessary to retreat. For food, there was
bean soup and coarse rice to which a few ounces of meat were
added each week. There was no work quota as such: instead,
energy was devoted to the cleaning of guns.

Shabby and unprofessional as their circumstances were, a
military complex was unmistakably keeping its eye on the
Ch'en-chou garrison. In addition to the population of five
thousand soldier families, there were twenty thousand soldiers.
An official conference rearranged their man to man formations
and group encampments. Several units were deployed down-
stream; other teams were assigned to mop up villages of bandits—
stragglers left over from the civil war.

Shen's troop soon departed for East Village, and arrived there
after seven grueling days by boat and three days on foot. Snipers
killed three of their men along the way. In retaliation, the troop
"executed" two thousand townspeople. Shen's tour of duty
lasted four months, a time fraught with military rigors and rural
barbarity. Market days were often enlivened by duels to the
death between villagers who slashed at each other with swords.
But perhaps the most remarkable incident as far as Shen was
concerned involved the young daughter of a trade union
chairman:

I stayed in East Village for four months. Two incidents occurred
that I will never forget. One was that often on market days, I would
see two villagers dueling with cutlasses until one of the two fell. The
other was that the younger daughter of the chairman of a trade
union, a girl who had died and been buried, was taken from her
grave that same day by a young man selling beancurd. He took

her body to a cave in the hills, and after having slept with her for
three days, returned her to her grave. Later, when the crime was
discovered, the beancurd seller was arrested and taken to our
Yamen. He was executed on the spot. A moment before the execution, his mind was still clear and unconfused. He did not shout for
food or drink. He did not curse, but only silently gazed at one of
his injured ankles. I asked him, "Who injured your foot?" He shook
his head. Then, as though he had recalled something amusing, he
smiled and gently said, "It rained that day. When I took her back,
I almost slipped into the coffin." I asked him again, "Why did you
do this?" He still smiled, looking at me as if I were a child who
did not understand love. He said nothing at first, but after a while
he spoke as though to himself, gently: "Very beautiful, very beautiful." Another soldier, therefore, said, "Lunatic, you're to be killed.
Aren't you afraid?" The man answered, "What's there to be afraid
of? Are you afraid to die?" The soldier was ashamed, and shouted,
"You son of a mad bitch, aren't you afraid to die? In a moment,
we'll cut your head off!" The man smiled faintly and said nothing.
The smile seemed to say, "You don't know which of us is mad."
I still remember this smile and have remembered it clearly all these
years.[4]

This slice of life later became a short story, "Three Men and
A Girl."

The army next transferred Shen to a garrison at Huai-hua
where he remained for a year and four months. Because he was
the only soldier in the entire corps who could read and write,
he was promoted to sergeant-clerk. Bureaucracy, however, seemed
a formality only, an afterthought, since the militiamen favored
blood to red tape. Perhaps because of his superiors' aversion
to "the law's delay," Shen the sergeant-clerk personally witnessed
seven hundred beheadings. The anger and disillusionment he
experienced in Huai-hua provided him with much that went
into the writing of "My Education." In this article, Shen was
to record in ink what he had seen in gore. Military power, he
wrote, was absolute power. Evidence of this was the intelligentsia
of Huai-hua who, while they lorded it over the masses, were
in turn subjugated by the soldiers. Slapped by a foot-soldier,
an aristocrat remained helpless, which led Shen to ponder the
role of the intellectual in a militarized society. Of what use
was an elite if any illiterate rifle bearer could step on one of

its members like a doormat? More and more, it appeared, the
only practical occupation was that of soldier—and that had
nothing to do with either reading or writing. Justice, or a vague
facsimile of it, was further removed from the letter of the law;
the sole authority was the army with its more "progressive"
interpretation of redress by bullet and chopping block.

No rationale could be found for this "education by killing," as
Shen was to write in his *Autobiography*. Looking back on these
experiences with bitterness, the former clerk would decry the
stupidity of mankind. Where he had been manacled by duty
and muzzled by despair, he now fought back with prose. His
Autobiography records the screams of slaughtered innocents.
It also records the stench of rotting flesh, and the follies that
lead to inhumanity.

Huai-hua was a microcosm of a civilization under siege. The
town had but six hundred houses, the largest functioning as an
assembly hall. Hot and dusty, its streets full of querulous folk,
Huai-hua might have been a replica of any frontier town in the
American Old West. It was here that Shen encountered what
might be called the felicities of human nature. A permanent
ludicrous fixture of Huai-hua was a forty-year-old prostitute:

> In front of the opium shop sat a woman of about forty: her rather
> flat face was thickly powdered, her plucked eyebrows thin lines;
> she would deliberately pull up her home-spun green trousers to reveal
> her pink stockings. When she saw soldiers and army cooks, she
> would turn away without so much as a glance to show how quiet and
> genteel she was, but if the passerby happened to be wearing the
> long gown of a gentleman, or the uniform of an officer, she would
> coquettishly smile and call out in a loving voice to the man in the
> house to do her a favor. When I walked by in the company of a
> private, I saw only her back. When I walked with the assistant
> battalion commander, I saw her face. At that time, I knew enough
> to appreciate such postures of human nature. I noticed this, but
> felt no ugliness, thinking that this is being "human." I have been
> very familiar with such "human affairs."[5]

Yet, there was more to Huai-hua than a finicky prostitute.
With no judicial elasticity, but with the rule of the sword to
settle all civic conflict, the army's presence could only impose

its own peculiar brand of equity. The killing never stopped. Estranged, and lacking any form of entertainment, soldiers occupied off-duty hours by watching their troop put civilians to death. These executions were performed in public, and were timed to provide daily spectacles for lonely soldiers who thus would have something to talk about over their wine and pork. Standing along the railing of a bridge, raw recruits made merry at the show, avidly studying the executioner's mastery of the big knife. To flaunt his swordsmanship, the executioner would frequently appropriate a butcher's table and chop off bits of pork to provide his captive audience with a snack. The soldiers themselves invented a new sport: pigball, a barbaric version of soccer. Contestants would kick a hog's head around until they were tired.

These explosions of animal energy, which were later to become one of his favorite story themes, proved too much for the sensitive Shen. At the marketplace, he would see what by then had become a commonplace of Huai-hua's moral landscape: a flank of soldiers and a boy carrying a pike, either end of which had pierced a human head. Long tutored in the perverse logic of army brass, Shen knew at once that the heads belonged to the boy's father and perhaps to one of his uncles. Still, the clerk reasoned, decapitation was at least a quicker, and in the final analysis, more merciful death than other, more brutal, forms of execution.

The daylight parades at the marketplace were nothing compared to the slow, agonizing tortures in the garrison at night. Inmates were beaten about the ankles with square pieces of iron until their bones were broken. Repeated beatings could knock the marrow from the bones of a foot; incense was filtered into the nose; iron rods bent shins; and there was the torch for a man's chest. Day after day, week after week, month after month, Shen had to sit at his desk, a perpetual witness in his official capacity as civil recorder. It was his duty to write down every last word and gasp of each prisoner being tortured in Huai-hua's private hell.

CHAPTER 3

The Butcher, the Printer, the Swaggerstick Maker

TO ALLEVIATE what had daily become a more gruesome situation, Shen the clerk took up calligraphy and diligently practiced his hand at it by an attic window. Introspective and somewhat diffident, the Hunan youth had had negligible contact with educated citizens, none at all with the literati. His social life, if it could be called that, had been restricted to barracks horseplay and private excursions into the countryside. Even if he had been inclined to fraternize with his fellow soldiers, or with local people, he would not have found much company. Relationships, whether army or civilian, were less than tenuous: they were illusory.

Happily, there was an individual stationed at Huai-hua who could offer Shen companionship. This was the battalion commander's new secretary. At first, Shen, who had been for most of his life exposed to brutes and laggards, was reserved. Interpreting the behavior as shyness, the secretary went about his business with disarming gentility. Shen was overwhelmed.

Behind the secretary's bland exterior resided a poet. Fervently, musically, he described the whistles of trains and steamboats, the magic of electricity (the telephone!), the quaintness of British and American military uniforms, the majesty of torpedo boats. For his part, Shen related many of his own experiences and impressions. Did the secretary know, he asked, that there was a difference between a tiger's roar and a wolf's bark. Did he know that it required a seasoned hunter to distinguish the tracks of a wild pig from the tracks of a goat? Inevitably, Shen's impressions of the life he had led were garish: the actual weight of a severed head, or the proper method for removing a man's gall bladder. The secretary introduced the clerk to the Chinese

encyclopedia, and to a newspaper called *Shen-pao*. The encyclopedia enlarged Shen's vocabulary; the newspaper to which
they both subscribed introduced Shen to the mainstream of
national affairs.

More pressing events, however, did not allow much time for
book-learning. The maintenance garrison at Huai-hua was ill-
equipped to fight the stronger insurgent forces threatening its
borders. Realizing his tactical danger, the troop commander
decamped his men and herded them back to Ch'en-chou. There,
the army was to remobilize for the advance on Szechwan. Because
he was too young to accompany the troops, Shen remained in
Ch'en-chou where he was assigned to copy reports. The work
seemed purposeless and life in the village was boring. The
monotony of his job dissipated the effects of his military training.
He missed Huai-hua and the encyclopedia, and he missed his
newspaper. To keep himself busy, he practiced calligraphy
until his eyes burned and his fingers were sore.

A year passed in this desultory manner. Then, from Szechwan
came news that their troop had met with heavy resistance and
was retreating to Hunan. A later wire confirmed the fears of
those who had been left behind in Ch'en-chou: the army had
been routed, the camp occupied, and every soldier, from the
commander to his secretary, had been killed in the battle. For
some time, the military had been a kind of sanctuary to Shen,
providing him with an opportunity to read encyclopedias and
subscribe to metropolitan dailies. Now, even those small luxuries
had been lost.

By August 1920, Shen was back in Hunan, discharged from
the army, with nothing but his severance pay to support him.
He found little to do. He could not re-enlist in the army. After
three months of indecision, Shen could stand it no longer, and
he set off on foot through the snow for Yüan-chou where he was
given lodgings by an uncle, a police chief. Here, the ex-soldier
was once again employed as a clerk. His job was to copy and
file violation tickets. Next to his office was the city jail. Each
night, Shen listened to the moans and screams of the inmates.
It was as though some malevolent god were replaying for him
the sounds of Huai-hua.

When the police force was assigned the task of collecting tax revenue from the Yüan-chou butchers, Shen was promoted to assistant tax collector. The irony of the situation did not escape Shen whose job was now to go from butcher's table to butcher's table, assessing the value of meat. Although his wages did not increase, the job liberated him from the dank jail and left him free to enjoy the comparative pleasures of a commercial world. Beyond the garrisons and prisons lay fresh water, nature's mat of leaves, everything in fact that was not hewn by sword or stained with blood. At home, Shen's uncle, the chief of police, wrote poems every day, as did many of his relatives. Calligraphy had been the clerk's poetry at Huai-hua; in Yüan-chou he discovered the original: he began to read all the poems he could find. More significantly, he got hold of Dickens' works in translation.

Shen changed. At seventeen, he was cultured and earned a respectable salary. From village squires, he learned how to write formal script and classical poetry. He received and rejected several marriage proposals from well-placed elders seeking a husband for their daughters. When Shen's mother and sisters learned of the young man's new life, they sold the old house in Hunan and moved at once to Yüan-chou.

Unhappily, the emergence of this new social personality did not entirely quash the impetuosity of the naïve Shen who knew nothing, or practically nothing, of the workings of the heart. Although he ignored haughtily protracted suits from what his family thought "more desirable quarters," he was smitten with a girl who, as it later developed, was more larcenous than loving.

In the heat and ignorance of young love, Shen dedicated amorous poems to his beloved which were relayed to her by her younger brother. If ever a season conspired successfully to fan such ardor, it was that languorous April with its peripheral civil war and threatening marauders in the hills. In the vise of romantic urgency, Shen neglected everything but his poetry. Having ingratiated himself, the brother who carried Shen's poem had begun borrowing sums of money from the lovesick poet's bank account. The day after, he would restore some, but not all the money. This odd arrangement continued for some time, until one morning the brother did not come to collect the new batch of love lyrics—whereupon Shen was notified by his bank that all his money was gone. The shock of front-line battle, the shock of abysmal prisons, had been overt manifestations of human cruelty engendered less by calculating minds than by animal energies; the shock of duplicity, on the other hand, was another sort of atrocity, the more atrocious, perhaps, because its cost was measured not in blood but in loss of faith and face. Disgraced and penniless, Shen was humiliated by the realization that he, too, in a sense, had been executed.

There was no alternative but to resign his post, leave his mother, sisters, and the several elders who had so eagerly sought him as a son-in-law. He moved on to Ch'ang-te. His old military outfit was quartered ninety miles away in neighboring T'ao-yüan. Because some of its ranking officers came from Hunan, acquaintances recommended Shen for a commission. But commissions were hard to obtain, and Shen had to content himself with occasional visits to T'ao-yüan where he had a cousin. Returning from these visits, he would write long, penitent letters to his mother. From her replies, he learned his former love had been abducted by a bandit chieftain and ransomed. Upon her release, she had married a Yünnan officer who soon after was killed by a sniper's bullet. Widowed, and thinking to expiate her sins, she had become a nun.

Shen had taken up lodgings in a small Ch'ang-te inn. The news from home depressed him. Even his cultural pursuits, calligraphy and poetry, afforded him little comfort. Despite the fact that for four months he subsisted on only thirty-six cents a day, Shen began to accumulate debts. Just when it seemed that he was bound for debtors' prison, a schooner carrying military uniforms docked upstream from Ch'ang-te. On board was one of his brother's friends, a dispatcher. To settle Shen's other obligations, a relative who had been a primary-school teacher went to see the innkeeper; the debts were canceled. Reprieved, Shen boarded the schooner.

It turned out to be quite an instructive journey. The dispatcher, twenty-five years old, was a salty though straightforward type who, by his own account, had slept with some forty different women. With an impish earthy humor, the dispatcher eloquently related anecdotes flavored with four-letter expletives. In this manner, the women he had wooed and won achieved, in the retelling, a special gloss. This street argot, peppered with puns, was to crop up in Shen's fiction, especially in his descriptions of the female body. Calligraphy had taught him the singular formalism of script; the encyclopedia had introduced him to language; aboard the schooner, Shen discovered idiom. He also discovered another character. A synthesis of the dispatcher would appear in a chapter of his *Random Sketches on a Trip to West Hunan.*

Once in Pao-ching, Shen was given shelter by a cousin, an army clerk. Hungry and without a job, Shen went from acquaintance to acquaintance, appearing unannounced at mealtime and leaving wordlessly after sharing whatever food was available. Pao-ching was not much different from many towns he had visited; its economy was backward, its people plain and poor. Nonetheless, the town had about it a special kind of optimism, and happily, the local garrison seemed more concerned with regional emancipation than with inquisition and extermination. Because the local commander was a man of high principles and devotion to duty, the troops were unusually industrious and well disciplined. These virtues were not lost on Shen, who, looking for a job, would dress up in his best uniform and, in borrowed shoes, belt and coat, seek out officers for an interview. Between interviews, he frequented his cousin's office, acquainting himself with the staff members and their chores, and helping out wherever and whenever there was a backlog of work to be done. This persistence finally paid off. One day, the chief secretary noticed him writing a letter for the office and inquired about the young man. Another clerk spoke up on the volunteer worker's behalf, explaining that Shen had been of considerable assistance to the staff for the last six months. This on-the-spot character reference was all that was necessary. Shen was offered a job at a salary of four dollars per month. Because he was an expert calligraphist, he made an exceptional clerk. But he was not content with what he knew and practiced his craft on his own. From his savings, he bought the latest editions on calligraphy, determined to absorb every facet of the ancients' art: "all forms of life nourished my soul, making it sparkle whenever it made contact with something."[1]

Several months passed as Shen bent over his desk, tracing,

balancing and embroidering his script. A promotion transferred him to the Advisory Bureau whose office was situated close to a hill decked with small tombs. Whenever he went uphill, Shen had to arm himself with a club. Packs of scavenger dogs and wolves prowled the cemetery for recently interred bodies, especially the bodies of infants which they could easily rend and devour. Rainy nights were particularly disquieting. Then, the hill would tremble with the baying of the packs, and the wind would howl, as though in response, and in protest against absolute loneliness.

The serenity of daylight, Shen thought, was a momentary illusion: there was always the night. He began to puzzle over metaphysical riddles. Death, he knew, belonged to the wormwood of the grave, and life must bear its living cross.

After ten months in Pao-ching, the Advisory Bureau was moved to Szechwan. Like refugees, the transfer unit filled the roads and highways, sleeping on benches, tables, and haystacks. A smaller group, Shen included, traveled deep into Szechwan, billeting at a place called Dragon Pool, an army camp where the men had nothing to do but distribute circulars and perform executions. Tenure in the army, however, was as unpredictable as the weather, and Shen was soon recalled to Hunan, there to become secretary to the officer who had been such a morale booster at Pao-ching.

Outwardly, the crude headquarters building squatting on a Hunan hill differed little from countless others Shen had worked in. What distinguished it was its conference room which had the appearance of a miniature museum. After office hours, Shen became both scholar and custodian of this room. Ecstatically, he studied *objets d'art*: old scroll paintings, and handicraft items of bronze and porcelain. Still more interesting was the conference room library where Shen discovered handbound books on history dating back to the successions of the Chinese dynasties. Each night, he would go over its five shelves of historical texts. Of this period and experience, Shen the poet was to write: "I began to have some idea of the art the Chinese people have created with a patch of color, a symmetry of lines, a piece of bronze, a handful of clay, a collage of words."[2]

Still, Shen longed for an intellectual relationship that had some degree of permanence. This desire was partially realized when an uncle settled across the river at a place known as Lion Cavern. Witty and wizened, the man was worth crossing the river for, and Shen listened attentively to his ramblings on the philosophy of the Sung and Yüan dynasties, interspersed with allusive names such as Yin-ming[3] and Ta-cheng,[4] and talk about the theory of evolution. To the young scholar, these were not airy tête-à-têtes, but meaningful sessions with an old master. Each lesson not only enriched significantly Shen's imagination, but intensified his loneliness: "At the time, I didn't know what was appropriate for me. I felt there had to be a goal, a career suitable to my character. But I couldn't decide just what it was, or how I could obtain it."[5]

As Shen began more and more often to visit his uncle at Lion Cavern, he became increasingly introverted, alienating himself from many of his acquaintances. He was moodier now, more remote, although he still kept in touch with four friends. Man Chen-hsien, who had read the complete works of Tseng Kuo-fan[6] and had always wanted to become a career soldier; T'ien-chieh, a classmate from his childhood; Lu-t'ao, a classmate from primary school and more recently a co-worker in the Advisory Bureau; Cheng Tzu-ts'an, Shen's boyhood friend, a Moslem. Two of Shen Ts'ung-wen's stories written at a later date are about Cheng and Lu-t'ao: "Black Night," and "In Memory of Lu-t'ao." Shen wrote, not only of his four friends, but of youth in general: "We considered our lives too commonplace, too peaceful, and not as they *should* have been. We wanted to venture out, try something novel, no matter how trivial. Even before understanding our choice, we had to make it—regardless of the consequences, for we would not complain about our fate."[7]

Fate, however, was not always kind. Man Chen-hsien was shot and killed in the 1929 Civil War; Cheng disappeared during another civil war. He had been graduated from the Whampo Military School; T'ien-chieh became a troop leader; and Lu-t'ao drowned in a river.

At Szechwan, in the meantime, the enterprising garrison commander from Pao-ching and Hunan was leading another mobilization drive. A new revenue department had just been established, and the army had ample provisions. Community spirit had never been higher. Local bureaucrats rallied the citizenry with the favorite slogan of the day: "Soldiers construct roads, plough the wilderness"; and programs: "Found schools" or "Build Factories." Next, the commander proposed to publish a magazine, and for this purpose, a huge printing press was purchased. Now, Shen had to double as chief proofreader and headquarters functionary. Virtually a live-in utility man for the newspaper, he had to share quarters with the shop foreman. The foreman, from Ch'ang-sha, Hunan, a man who was very much concerned with the literary revolution known as the May Fourth Movement, had a considerable influence on the proofreader-clerk. He, too, was a student of literature, and because he was older than Shen, had many valuable experiences to share. He spoke of great happenings to the west of Hunan, of poets new to the public and new to Shen, of the effectiveness of profound thought in the writing of essays. The foreman also communicated to Shen a passion for periodicals, singling out *Creation Weekly*,[8] edited by Kuo Mo-jo, which the proofreader began to read in earnest. It was by reading many other newspapers and magazines that Shen learned to differentiate between the literary style and the vernacular, or *pai-hua*. More important, the foreman insisted, was thought. Ironically, Shen would in the future be put on the defensive by critics who charged him with being a "thoughtless writer. "I didn't understand what thought was," Shen was later to write, "and felt ashamed. If I had anticipated that ten years later my essays and stories would be criticized as thoughtless by so-called critics who could not read the verbal nuances in my pieces, I would not have felt ashamed when I heard the foreman talking about 'thought.' "[9]

Though few in number, the foreman's books constituted a library for Shen. Initially, though, reading critical treatises filled him with rancor. He wondered why people, and well-known writers at that, always carped about human behavior. To him, it seemed the critics' resolutions were as subjective as the values they attacked. But the freshness of such periodicals as *Hsin Ch'ao* (*New Tide*) and *Kai-tsao* (*Reconstruction*) eventually converted the anticritic, who, in his later works, joined the ranks of social arbiters.

At army headquarters, the workload had become so great that Shen had to quit his job with the newspaper and return to his former job as army clerk. Then, a high fever confined him to bed for forty days. His convalescence was marred by news of Lu-t'ao's death. The stout, devil-may-care Lu-t'ao had wagered a friend that he could swim a mile-wide river, and had drowned in the currents. Four days later, his body was recovered. Still weak from his sickbed, Shen paid his last respects. His friend's death resurrected for Shen the question of man's mortality. Wholesale butchery had dogged his heels ever since he had entered the army; but the single death of a friend was somehow hauntingly symbolic, as the mass executions had been memorably insane. Disoriented once more, Shen was resolved to move on, farther away, perhaps to a new world where he could determine his own fate. He decided to go to Peking and enroll as a student in the university.

It was the winter of 1922. The May Fourth Movement had just subsided. The proofreader and clerk was twenty years old.

CHAPTER 4

Political Metamorphoses

IN 1842, just a year before the Opium War (the Anglo-Chinese
War), China began to undergo a series of changes. The cry
for *wei-hsin* and *ke-ming* (reform and revolution) punctuated
almost every decade in the latter half of the nineteenth century.
Regarding these demands, Huang Tsun-hsien (1848-1905), the
last poet of the Ch'ing Dynasty and consul general to Japan,
Singapore, and San Francisco from the 1880's to the 1890's made
this prediction: "The changes in China are inevitable adapta-
tions of Western systems; all this will come to be thirty years
from now...."[1] In 1860, French and British allies comprising the
Anglo-French Military Expedition broke into the Forbidden
City and put the Yüan-ming-yüan (Summer Palace) to the torch,
burning with it the old "closed-door" policy. Resident scholar-
officials were rudely awakened to the fact that to save their
country from Western imperialism, their people would have to
be "westernized," culturally and militarily. In 1861, the *Tsungli
Yamen* (Foreign Office) was established in Peking; its express
purpose was to show that the Ch'ing dynasty had sufficient
flexibility to accommodate such delicate matters as international
relations. In the same year, the T'ung-wen-kuan or Foreign
Language Institute was organized; and this resulted in large
scale translation of books on political thought and western technology. Tseng Kuo-fan, Tso Tsung-t'ang, and Li Hung-chang
initiated a mobilization drive focused on the building of ship-
yards and the establishment of new military schools. Between
1872 and 1876, many students were sent abroad for "Western
exposure." Upon their return to China, many of these scholars
helped promulgate various reforms.

Japan's victory in the Battle of Chia-wu in 1895 encouraged
K'ang Yu-wei to head a Chinese political reform movement in

China, in 1898. The reform movement proved to be a failure after only one hundred days (from July to September, 1898), and its disciples fled to Japan or were executed. This idealistic movement reactivated numbers of intellectuals who were then to catalyze the Revolution of 1911—a revolution which could be taken as the culmination of the tumultuous discontent in the empire after the 1900 Boxer Uprising. Professor Chow Tse-tsung has summed up the critical atmosphere in his book, *The May Fourth Movement*:

Party politics were tried for the first time in the Republic, under the manipulation of warlords. In 1914 Parliament was dissolved and the constitution was annulled by the warlord president Yüan Shih-k'ai. In 1915 and 1917 two unsuccessful monarchical restoration movements were staged. Yüan's abolition of the Republic lasted eighty-three days and the restoration of the Manchu boy Emperor to the throne by Chang Hsün, the *tuchun* of Anhwei Province, ended in twelve days after Chang's pigtailed troops in Peking were disbanded. Thereafter, while the whole country was in fact controlled by local competing *tuchuns*, the power of the central government was left in the hands of Tuan Ch'i-jui, the warlord who was Yüan's long-time subordinate. Tuan was the leader of the Anfu Club, a political group of warlords and bureaucrats with Japanese financial support. To oppose the Peking regime, Sun Yat-sen established the rival Military Government in Canton on September 1, 1917. From this time on, a number of indecisive civil wars between the North and the South stirred the country.[2]

It was estimated that between 1915 and 1922 no less than ten major civil wars were waged by the warlords. To fortify their own selfish ambitions, some of the warlords cooperated with foreign governments in the outright sale of Chinese natural resources. While a few students looked to the West for intellectual armament, local entrepreneurs pillaged the land. Caught in the middle was the common man with nothing to hold on to but dreams and promises:

. . . he who paid the bill was the Chinese peasant. Intermittent fighting and the cruelty, the hunger that came with it, provided the permanent background of his daily existence. His son was carried off to make war and much of his produce was taken away in taxes.

Such arbitrariness in everyday life turned him into an exhausted and dispirited man. His refuge was in a silent, but passionate nationalism. . . . Far above his head, kaleidoscopic political changes produced more or less ephemeral governments.[3]

With the outbreak of World War I, foreign powers had more to occupy them than China, who was left alone to solve her problems, not least of which was the deterioration of her agrarian economy. There followed a long dry spell of reassessment and experimentation. Then, with the end of the war, foreign attention focused once more on China, and once more it became necessary for Chinese intellectuals to discover a cultural ideal round which the masses might rally.

Chancellor Ts'ai Yüan-p'ei of Peking University gathered around him the most influential scholars representing the old and new schools. From the academic coalition thus formed, the new school produced a new magazine, *New Youth,* whose goal was "to transplant the terms of Western ideology into the thought of China," and thereby "create a new vernacular literature." Its issues were devoted to "spirited debates over such questions as centralism versus federalism in politics or the real relation between science and philosophy of life."

The first issue carried editor Ch'en Tu-hsiu's "Call to Youth" which strongly criticized the archaic and the rotten in Chinese society:

I only, with tears, place my plea before the young and the vital, in the hope that they will achieve self-awareness, and begin to struggle. What is this self-awareness? It is to be conscious of the value and responsibility of one's young life and vitality, to maintain one's self respect, which should not be sacrificed: and what is the struggle? It is to exert one's intellect, discard resolutely the old and the rotten, regard them as enemies; and as the flood, or as savage beasts, keep away from their neighborhood and refuse to be contaminated by their poisonous germs.[4]

For Ch'en Tu-hsiu, youth meant not only "shining hair, smooth countenances, strong backs and broad chests," but a vigorous and probing mentality. To help the young escape the clutches of the old and the decadent, he proposed six principles:

1. Be independent, not servile.
2. Be progressive, not conservative.
3. Be aggressive, not retiring.
4. Be cosmopolitan, not isolationist.
5. Be utilitarian, not formalistic.
6. Be scientific, not imaginative.[5]

The popular clamor for rejuvenation inevitably identified the totem of all that was formal and conservative in China: Confucianism. Irreverently, systematically, *New Youth* itemized the debilities and debilitating effects of Confucianism on its adherents in such articles as "A Discussion of Confucius," "Constitution and Confucianism," and "On the Way of Confucius and Modern Life." The following three points comprise a list of then current objections to Confucianism:

1. Confucianism is the product of a feudal society, the units of which are made up of families and clans, not individuals.

2. Confucianism preaches noncompetitiveness of spirit, thus making it unfit for a modern, competitive society.

3. Confucianism is non-religious, thus it should not be made a state religion, as proposed by K'ang Yu-wei.[6]

Such hostility toward Confucianism angered traditional scholars who deemed themselves the guardians of Chinese "national essence" (*Kuo-ts'ui*). They in turn lodged charges against *New Youth* for "destroying old ethics (loyalty, filial piety, chastity), destroying old art (Chinese opera), destroying old politics (privileged rule)."[7] Ch'en Tu-hsiu did not deny the charges, but replied that such crimes were committed in the interest of advocating science and democracy. To further illustrate his point and perhaps also to twit his critics, he wrote: "We are convinced at present that only these two gentlemen (Mr. Science and Mr. Democracy), can cure the dark maladies in Chinese politics, morality, learning and thought."[8]

New Youth did not limit itself to frontal attacks on the Old Order, however. As a part of its intellectual expansion, it also published translations of, and introductions to men such as Ibsen, Darwin, Spencer, Turgenev, Dostoevski, Adam Smith, Schopenhauer, J. S. Mill, Huxley, Nietzsche, and Rousseau. In 1917, Hu Shih returned from the United States to Peking. As a

philosophy student at Columbia University he had often engaged in various discussions concerning the Chinese language
and the possibility of literary reform in China. Following his
return, he published in *New Youth* the article "Some Tentative
Suggestions for the Reform of Chinese Literature," which
advocated a liberation of Chinese writing from its old forms and
hackneyed uses, and the restoration of the vernacular. Hu Shih
elaborated on these views in another piece, "Constructive Literary Revolution: A Literature of National Speech—A National
Speech of Literary Quality." To achieve a potent literary revolution, he pointed out, Chinese writers must work solely within the
boundaries of their national heritage—the national language—
and thereby build a *living* literature. This theoretical attack
struck many traditional writer-critics, and even Hu Shih's contemporaries in America, as radical. In support of Hu Shih,
Ch'en Tu-hsiu wrote:

In China we have undertaken three revolutions, and yet darkness has not disappeared from the scene. This is partly because these
revolutions each had "the head of a tiger but the tail of a snake."
They began well enough, but were never carried to the logical con-
clusions. The old dirt was not washed by blood. But the major
cause of the continued prevalence of darkness in China is the fact
that even that kind of revolution "with a tiger's head and a snake's
tail" has not been carried out by us in the fields of ethics, morality,
literature and fine arts, which, laden with a great deal of debris
and covered by a thick, dark smoke-screen, are the sources of our
spiritual life. That is why the purely political revolution is incapable
of changing our society. The fundamental cause of all these failures
lies in the fact that we are afraid of revolution and ignorant of its
function in the improvement of civilization.[9]

Opposition from diehard scholastics was immediate, although
more hysterical than concentrated. A faction at Peking University
argued that Chinese classical literature would always be valid
inasmuch as it imparted *Taoism* which was, after all, the "Law
of Life." Didacticism then, according to this point of view, was
preferable to "realism." And *wen-yen* (literary language) was
more flexible than the vernacular *pai-hua* (language of the
people). The language controversy raged for two years before

New Youth and its "radicals" began in 1918 to publish exclusively in *pai-hua*. A year later, more than four hundred new magazines adopted the vernacular. And then on January 12, 1920, the Ministry of Education issued an ordinance which made the language of the people, *pai-hua*, the official language.

While literary activists were hotly debating the emancipation of Chinese letters, the country's problematical foreign relations were far from decided. Diverted by the European War, Western powers had relegated their interests in China to Japan, who compelled the Tuan Ch'i-jui government to sign an agreement in 1915 which, among other things, called for Japanese control of Manchuria, Inner Mongolia, Shantung (China's northeast province), and the Yangtze Valley. The effect of acceptance of these demands would be the Japanese colonization of these areas and economic and administrative control of the whole country. On May 7, 1915, after four months of negotiations, Japan sent China an ultimatum. Yüan Shih-k'ai signed an agreement which permitted Japan all its demands, except the last: control of China's government, finances, police and national defense, and the building of vital railway lines connecting the provinces of Hupeh, Kiangsi, and Kwangtung.

Despite the Japanese demands for secrecy, the Tuan Ch'i-jui government made the stipulations of the agreement known to the public through the press, whose protest stirred up nationalist and anti-warlord sentiments. The cruelest blow of all, however, came on April 30, 1919, when Woodrow Wilson, Lloyd George, and Clemenceau formed the Council of Four and secretly agreed upon the transfer to Japan of all German interests in Shantung, thus making a mockery of the presence of the Chinese delegates to the Paris Peace Conference. This triggered the 1919 May Fourth Movement, a day of wrath and protest for thousands of students who rampaged through the streets of Peking, shouting their betrayal and clamoring for reform. The furor of these demonstrations was such that the government was forced to capitulate; officials in key positions were made to resign or were summarily dismissed; and, most important of all, on June 28, China refused to sign the peace treaty with Germany. Not only did the May Fourth Movement embarrass the Western powers, and "internationalize" China, but it also revitalized, from within, the country's intellectual atmosphere. Before the nationwide rallies and marches, China's renaissance was but an idealistic concept among various intellectuals, the secret fruit of which was either unknown or inaccessible to the masses. With the student demonstrations dormancy came to an end. Now, such magazines as *New Youth* and *The Renaissance* were joined in the literary revolution by *New Tide,* and the country was inundated with the sudden appearance of more than four hundred different periodicals, all pursuing the same line. Student activism, too, had allied teachers, laborers, and merchants, developing the power of the people, encouraging them to free themselves from the constraints of conventions and to express dissatisfaction with the existing conditions. Regardless of how remote the authorities seemed, the May Fourth Movement proved that mass indignation could not be ignored. Moreover, having witnessed the width and breadth, and the depth, of her self-determination, foreign powers could not then, and perhaps ever again, take China for granted.

However sweet this triumph was initially, it left a pungent aftertaste. Many successful revolutions are ultimately self-congratulatory, and this was the case with the May Fourth Movement. Having defined the objectives of the literary revolution, some of its leaders were now ready to branch out, and divisiveness became a problem. Ch'en Tu-hsiu had been arrested by the authorities on June 11, 1919, while distributing handbills and leaflets. Upon his release shortly thereafter, he sought to convert *New Youth* and make it a political mouthpiece. Although his editorial board had supported him without reservation at the height of the literary impasse, they now rejected Ch'en's proposals. By the end of the year, Ch'en was in Shanghai, single-handedly organizing the New Youth Society and editing *New Youth.* Turning then to the left, Ch'en founded the Chinese Communist Party. *New Youth* was to suffer drastically with this shift in ideology: the post office confiscated it, and contributions stopped coming in. In Kwangtung, Ch'en wrote to Hu Shih for advice. Once partisans in the literary revolution, the two were now separated by an ideological gap. Undaunted, Ch'en moved on to Canton where he set up the *New Youth Quarterly.* Its first edition was a special on International Communism. Through its several suborgans, *New Youth* thus declared its Communist principles. To widen the breach between the intellectuals, Hu Shih printed *Endeavor Weekly*, a liberal tabloid published in Peking, in May 1922. The literary dispute and the question of language were now fully a part of much larger political issues.

CHAPTER 5

Apprenticeship in Peking

IN the winter of 1922, Shen arrived in Peking with twenty-seven dollars to his name: his new home, a riverside sawdust inn, west of the city. Ting Ling,[1] who was to become Shen's lifelong friend, described Peking as "the old capital, a city for learning, a city of culture." Here, one bought or borrowed a copy of *Morning Post: Literary Supplement* to read the latest works of eminent figures. Apartment-based university students thrived on Goethe, Heine, Byron, Keats, and Lu Hsün. Or they idled away hours exchanging views on Maupassant, Chekhov, Ibsen, Shakespeare, Gorky, and Tolstoi. The students passed their time browsing in secondhand bookstores, dining leisurely at cheap restaurants, making individual pilgrimages to scenic spots, or meeting friends. Lives were devoted to absorbing historical China, to writing poetry and to contributing thoughtful little essays to journals. It was the best of Parisian bohemia, without the inhibiting presence of political regimes.

Shen knew, however, that all China was not cozy undergraduate small talk. Questioned by a relative as to what he was doing in Peking, Shen replied that he was there for his ideals, and for study. Which ideals? the relative wanted to know. Which books? Only by militancy or obsequiousness could a professor wheedle his thirty-six dollars a month. Bookworms? They were doomed to read dead books and to study themselves to death. Their future in education was no better than the soldier's in the army. But Shen recalled the ten thousand farmers he had seen slain, and he felt again the bond of stupidity linking oppressor and oppressed. He could forgive neither the killers' remorselessness nor the victims' docility. He had seen villagers coerced, cajoled, crucified, and all he had ever heard them say was: "You kill my body, but I corrupt your soul."

So Shen had begun to read *New Youth, New Tide,* and *Reconstruction.* His study led him to believe that before any kind of social reformation could evolve, contemporary literature would have to be upgraded. A nation's sensibility, he believed, was sapped by avarice and the indiscriminate abuse of power. For a man to subscribe personally to this reality of warlords and killings and opium diets meant to embrace the entire utilitarian ethic. These, he said, were some of his reasons for leaving the army.

The skeptical relative was impressed. Here was a not so young man who had yet to master the new punctuation, prepared to challenge the system's multiheaded dragon. Equipped with medieval fancies and an almost staggering faith in himself, Shen was prepared to challenge the conscience of Peking.

As far as the city was concerned, Shen was just another shadowy figure dogging its labyrinthine alleys. That winter, he lived without heat and often without food for two or three days at a time. His contributions to newspapers and magazines came back almost as fast as he sent them out. Once, in desperation, he joined a shabby parade of halfhearted military recruits. Bearing a smudged white banner, Shen, along with other ungainly "volunteers," shuffled in shame and defeat along the Heavenly Bridge in Peking City. When it came time to sign the recruit's contract which would entitle each man to what amounted to a beggar's ration, Shen left in fury and disgust. He returned to his small unheated room at the Tsing-hua Apartments.

Working at night, Shen wrote an essay for which the *Morning Post* paid him fifty cents. This was a pittance, but it meant bread. The hardest times were over. Shen's articles began to appear regularly in the *Morning Post* under the pseudonym, Hsiu Yün-yün. Periodic vouchers (usually four to twelve dollars) were meager, but they provided him with his most basic needs.

Gradually, Shen the journalist was making himself known among Peking's intellectuals. His next contact was with Hu Yeh-p'in, the editor of *People's Literature,* a literary supplement of the *Peking Press.* A little older than Shen, Hu Yeh-p'in[2] was destined to become one of the five martyrs in the "Reign of White Terror"[3] in Shanghai. He had attended Navy School at Fukien but had moved on to Peking when the school was closed due to financial difficulties. Shen's work for *People's Literature* was impressive enough to merit a visit from its editor. In Shen's "narrow and moldy study" the frustrated navy officer and the "retired" soldier had much to talk about. One chilly morning, Hu brought along a young woman who introduced herself simply as "Ting." Her round face was enhanced by long eyebrows; she wore a gray jacket and a short green linen skirt. At first she stood quietly in the doorway; then she sat down, smiling. Ting's real name, Shen learned, was Chiang Ping-tzu. She had been born in West Hunan, close to Shen's hometown. At that time, he could not know that in half a decade this unprepossessing visitor was to become the most talked-about woman writer in China. For the next ten years, Shen was a trusted friend of Hu and Ting. Unhappily, the relationship did not endure intellectual disaffections: Hu and Ting became increasingly committed to political causes, whereas Shen, whose literary interests lay elsewhere, did not.

Ting's circumstances in 1923, however, were no better than Shen's. She was unemployed, and she was not a university student. She had combed the bustling streets of the city for opportunities and possibilities. Her room was dingy, with a damp earthen floor and strips of board for a bed. She stuffed the cracks in the walls with paper, and on the window shades sketched profiles of human figures. Uninhabitable as the room seemed to Shen, Ting appeared to be relaxed, even happy in it.

In April, Shen went to work for the West Hill library on the West Hill of the Peking suburbs. His short fiction at this time was sharply critical of overbearing superintendents ("Cotton Shoes") and of a standoffish gentility ("The Sorrows of a Baboon"). These two stories displeased Shen's employer who cautioned the young man against writing further social criticism. Nettled, Shen later responded in his *In Reminiscence of Hu Yeh-p'in* in which, at one point, he decried servitude and parasitism as the principal worms clogging the intestines of society. Official interdiction did little to diminish Shen's natural critical tendencies. Next, he began to write vernacular poetry, the form which had become so effective a literary tool after the May Fourth Movement.

August was reunion time with Hu and Ting who were living together, posing as man and wife. The couple made up for their poverty with bright chatter and ambitious plans. They described for Shen the plans they had to publish a magazine, to be called *Red and Black*, which was to appear several years later when all three were in Shanghai. At the moment, however, Hu and Ting needed decent lodgings. Shen referred them to an apartment house, west of Peking, where he himself had lived before moving to West Hill. It was a fortuitous arrangement: the apartment manager was a patron of sorts, one who had been acquainted with other men of letters living at one time or another in his house.

Now, Shen, Hu, and Ting were practically neighbors. When they got together to talk, it was always of the proposed magazine. According to Peking statistics, a thousand copies of a magazine printed in the size and format of *Yu-ssu Weekly* would require capital of only twelve dollars per issue, which was very little, especially when one had to consider the psychological debts incurred by a freelance writer contributing to newspapers and magazines. There just was no weekly or supplement in which a beginning writer could publish his work on a regular basis. Complicating matters were the individual biases involved: while most editors openly favored contributions from those who had some kind of reputation, many writers thought twice before contributing to magazines which they suspected had a high mortality rate in beginners' contribution. Authors who took the risk found themselves waiting in vain for either an acceptance or a rejection slip. In many cases, editors did not even bother to acknowledge contributions. Another problem was that a large majority of writers submitted first drafts for acceptance. Owing to an astonishing lack of professionalism in Peking's editorial world, reams of manuscripts were consigned to limbo—misplaced, thrown out, or burned. Shen's *In Reminiscence of Hu Yeh-p'in* recounted how one-third of his own early works were lost. But, *Yu-ssu Weekly* was no ordinary magazine. When Shen finished his short story "Fu Sheng," Hu personally handed the manuscript to Chou Tso-jen, *Yu-ssu*'s editor and the younger brother of Lu Hsün. The story was published in June, 1925, and a proud Hu immediately presented Shen with a copy of *Yu-ssu*.

In 1925, Hu and Ting returned to Hunan. Shen left his position at the West Hill library to work as a dispatcher for the

Modern Critic. From Hunan, Hu mailed poems which Shen submitted for publication in either *Modern Critic* or *Morning Post: Literary Supplement*. Shen himself was slowly building a reputation through contributions to magazines which survived the Nationalist onslaught against the conservative royalists in the capital. Many weeklies and literary supplements were dying or were being moved to Shanghai.

When Hu and Ting returned to Peking, Shen periodically shared quarters with them. In 1926, the Nationalist Expedition[4] army advanced northward into the city, forcing all printing enterprises to move to Wuhan, Hupeh, where life was more peaceful and conducive to the trade. It seemed that the past was catching up with Shen as the Nationalist Expedition marched into Nanking. He had visions of mass exodus, of inquisitions, of bloodshed. But, despite these fears, Shen remained with Hu and Ting in Peking. That same year, the Pei-hsin Press brought out Shen's first book, *The Ducks*, a collection of stories, prose pieces, one-act plays and some poetry. The pieces had been written when the author was on the verge of starvation. Taken as a whole, the works showed a simplicity of style, a keenness of insight. It also revealed the author's preference for the Hunan dialect and an autobiographical use of his army experience. If his language did not have the firmness and resonance of his later writings, it nonetheless cast a harsh light on his characters, who were prose facsimiles of Hunan peasants.

At best, life in Peking had been one disenchantment after another. All big cities, Shen discovered, were alike in their selfish exploitation of the innocent. All a man had to do was to look over his shoulder to see the disengaged, the disoriented, the permanently damaged, the eternally damned. Contrary to Ting Ling's portrait of literati and the university town, Shen saw in Peking a beast feeding on the rootless young to sustain a corrupt and corrupting system. For his own roots, Shen looked to Hunan, to the aboriginal tribes, and even to his more pleasant memories of army life. However, it was the hunger, hostility, disillusionment, and bitterness he had experienced in Peking that provided the substance of *The Ducks*.

CHAPTER 6

Shanghai: 1927

IN April, 1927, Shen sailed to Shanghai where the editorial board of *Modern Critic* had moved. He found attic lodgings on Shan-chung Lane in the French Concession. The room was simply furnished, with a wooden bed, chair, and desk. His writing at this time was prolific, and his reputation growing.

In September, 1927, Shen's second book of short stories was published by Crescent Moon Press. Encouraged by the modest success of New North Press (Pei-hsin Press) which had published Shen's first collection, other Shanghai publishers followed suit: Modern Press, Spring Tide Press, Fu-tan Press, Water Foam Press, K'ai-ming Press all began to publish works by various writers. Throughout Shanghai, the printing-publishing business was booming. Some enterprises, of course, folded almost immediately; others, however, flourished, most notably the K'ai-ming Press. However poorly they were paid for the stories they submitted, Shen, Hu, and Ting flooded the new publishers with manuscripts. For Shen in particular, the memory of real poverty was disturbingly fresh. In his *The Non-dead Diary*, he wrote of a coat he had had made that was taken by his relatives. He ordered another coat, except that this time he did not have the money to pay for it. The tailor came around several times to collect, and Shen had no alternative but to tell him to resell the coat for the money he owed him. By August, 1928, Shen had left his attic room for the Mountain Ling-yin, or Hermit Mountain, near West Lake. There, he stayed in a cabin on what was called Shih-shun Peak.

Meanwhile, a kind of intellectual tug-of-war was threatening to divide China's literary scene. Caught between the rival schools of proletarian literature on the one hand and individualistic literature on the other, Shen tried to stay out of the dispute,

51

even though he had been identified with the Crescent Moon School, headed by Hsü Chih-mo and Hu Shih, both of whom considered him "one of theirs." It was also a time of factions and literary cliques. The Literary Research Association, organized in 1921, in Peking, and managed principally by Chou Tso-jen, Shen Yen-ping (Mao Tun), Cheng Chen-to, and Yeh Shao-chün, was one of the most prestigious. Mao Tun later went to Shanghai to edit *Fiction Monthly* which eventually became the Association magazine as sponsored by the Commercial Press. *Times News* in Shanghai published a literary supplement twice a week, under the editorship of Cheng Chen-to. This became an Association bi-weekly. When Mao Tun resigned his post at *Fiction Monthly,* Cheng succeeded him. Since all the magazines were based in Shanghai, the Literary Association had to move there. Not unlike an exclusive religious movement, the Literary Research Association was soon solidly entrenched. Its successions to power came from within. The majority of the reading public regarded its writings as Holy Writ. In tone and general philosophy, the writings it sponsored were largely didactic, advocating realistic literature or art for life's sake. The Association took a very dim view of the whimsical or romantic. It attacked poets who still indulged in "literary language." The vanguard of the association were concerned with issues, not with ideals; meat, matter, substance—Life. So narrow an attitude naturally provoked hostile reaction.

The opposition which called itself the Creation Society was organized in July, 1921, and was soon just as solidly entrenched. The principal leaders of Creation Society were Kuo Mo-jo, Ch'eng Fang-wu and Yü Ta-fu. In 1922, Yü Ta-fu singlehandedly published *The Creation Quarterly* which folded after only a few issues. The following year, the first issue of *Creation Weekly* came out, and a literary supplement in *China News* appeared with contributions from poets like Feng Chih, Wen I-to, and Liang Shih-ch'iu. By 1925, Yü Ta-fu had had a falling out with Kuo Mo-jo and Ch'eng Fang-wu, and left the Society. When Kuo Mo-jo joined the army to take part in the Northern Expedition against the warlords, the society was further weakened. It was not long before the Communist propagandists enjoying the editorial vacuum began to publish *Creation Monthly, Flood,*

Quicksand, and *Cultural Criticism,* thinly disguised revolutionary pamphlets advertising the new ideology. What had started
as a purely romantic lode had become an organ of revolution.

The third group to oppose the Literary Research Association
was the Crescent Moon Society led by Hu Shih and Hsü
Chih-mo. The name of their group had been inspired by a collection of poems by Rabindranath Tagore whom Hsü Chih-mo
had met when the poet was visiting China in 1924. In 1925, Hsü
edited the literary supplement of the Peking *Morning Post;* a
year later, the Crescent Moon Society was founded. Its original
members included Hu Shih, Liang Shih-ch'iu, Lo Lung-chi,
Hsü Chih-mo, and Wen I-to, most of whom had studied either in
Great Britain or America. Thereafter they were called the Anglo-
American clique. Shen Ts'ung-wen who had begun publishing in
the Peking *Morning Post: Literary Supplement,* became a friend
of Hu Shih and Hsü Chih-mo. A major outlet for the society was
its very own *Modern Critic,* founded in 1924 by Ch'en Hsi-ying.
On March 10, 1928, Hu Shih, Hsü Chih-mo, Liang Shih-ch'iu and
Lo Lung-chi founded the *Crescent Moon Monthly* with Hsü
Chih-mo and Lo Lung-chi serving as editors-in-chief. They
stressed the importance of "health" and "dignity" in writing as
opposed to sentimentality, decadence, aestheticism, didacticism,
political propaganda and pornography. Essentially, the Society
avoided political commitments, left or right. And it was with
this group—one which demanded neither political collaboration
or literary direction, only quality, that Shen felt himself most at
home.

In the autumn of 1928, P'eng Hao-hsü, editor-in-chief of the
Shanghai Central Daily News and a respected staffer of *Modern
Critic* was looking for someone to edit the literary supplement
of the *Daily News.* Shen, who had gone to the north of China
to spend a few months with his ailing mother, came back to
Shanghai. At that time, Shen, Hu, and Ting were deeply involved
in their own enterprise, *Red and Black,* another literary supplement. From the newspaper itself the three were earning two
hundred dollars a month. While the political situation seemed
precarious, their involvement was not without its own success.
Red and Black became the nucleus of the *Red and Black
Monthly.* Perhaps it was this courageous effort in the face of

odds that spurred the Human World Bookstore to engage Shen, Hu and Ting to edit its own monthly periodical. The three borrowed whatever money they could and set up their own publishing house. They moved to a street in the French Concession. Here, they edited the *Red and Black Literary Supplement,* the *Human World Monthly,* and their own magazine, *Red and Black Monthly.* Hu handled the proofreading, sent manuscripts to the press, procured printing materials, and acted as all-purpose agent, making the rounds of bookstores to check on sales and promotion. Once the magazines had been printed, Shen and Ting took care of the mailing and general distribution in the city. The first issue of *Red and Black Monthly* came out early in 1929. A week after its publication, a thousand copies had been sold in Shanghai alone. There were many letters of encouragement from different parts of the country.

In the meantime, the Creation Society had become pronouncedly Communist. Their new slogan was "Literature is the tool for class struggle!" Editor Lu Hsün rallied the opposition with *The Torrent,* a magazine in whose editorials he strongly criticized "proletarian revolutionary literature," accusing its standard bearers of naïveté. Liang Shih-ch'iu made it a three cornered fight with his "Art of Scoff" in *Crescent Moon Monthly.* Shen, Hu, and Ting looked on disdainfully. Of the struggle, Shen wrote: "Tendency (meaning commercial interest) is not what we want to bring up so as to benefit our own clique. We have no determination other than the wish to try our best. We hope the magazine will sell copies, but we do not want to lower our standards to achieve that end."[1]

To the three partners, but mostly to Shen, literature was based on life. In *In Reminiscence of Hu Yeh-p'in,* he wrote:

Literature is something which can take on wings of imagination and fly to another world. It does not lack the widest freedom, and it allows one's emotions to take a promenade through all phenomena. Whoever wishes to fly to the past world for a rest, whoever wishes to fly to the future world for a rest, does not have to confine his own movements because of the tastes of his own time. If he feels that in rectifying the mistakes of all the systems of society he must do something more positive, he does not lack the right. He has every right, but he is not obliged to succumb to any fashionable taste. What is plausible to him is his honesty in his work, and the achievement of his diligence."[2]

Because of their convictions, Shen, Hu, and Ting were more or less isolated from their contemporaries. It appeared that to stay in business and therefore in the national conscience and consciousness, they must choose to side either with the proletarian literature of the Communists or the national literature of the nationalists. Book merchants were quite understandably cheered by the situation. Topicality was not only a healthy commodity, it was good for business. Shen and his two partners soon discovered that their convictions were not enough, that selling books required more than good intentions.

The *Human World Monthly* folded after its fourth issue; the *Red and Black Monthly* after its eighth issue, in September, 1929. Shen was not surprised. He had foreseen the end. Like handwriting on the very fragile wall of Chinese letters, he had read the predictions of his competitors, he had heard the voices of the merchant complex telling him that only money had any value, that paper was paper unless it also happened to be currency.

Shen's frustrations at this time are expressed in *In Reminiscence of Ting Ling*:

In order to point out the corruption and fallacy of this nation, this society, to rectify all the mistakes of this social system which should not go on, why shouldn't literature be fixed in one direction so that it can be a lever, a thunder, a storm? Literature naturally allows people to calculate such effect. Although it cannot unify all writers of different attitudes, other writers who have seen clearly the fixed direction can persist in their own clear faith. . . .

. . . More than half of the publication enterprises controlled by the merchants along this coast tend to mold all writers according to different vogues and fashions to attract writers, readers, and to make a profit. Thus, our new Chinese literature, for the past ten years, excluding those unmentionable new Shanghai school writers and those opportunists who change incessantly, has swollen up with a leisure class who live the way they do mainly by sustaining the Shanghai merchants and some irascible professors in the universities. Together, they constitute clowns in various postures. They originated those tedious quarrels and idled away ten precious years in their so-called struggle. In those ten years, the same professors became famous and retained their stubbornness by arguing that there is still no Shakespeare, no Tolstoi, in China. And the famous leisure class, with their rumors and slander, hobble into old age. The smarter ones find other trades. Some are reluctant to grow old. Upright and indestructible, they justify their existence with shallow careers and inchoate ideals. Ah, but there they still are, standing erect, at the forefront—the pillars of society. Because they always chart progress on a profit basis, they abhor taking up a pen to write something that would approximate their old ideals: nor can they apply any systematic theory by which they can pinpoint their forms and content and know what method and hope are needed to produce their so-called Chinese monumental writing. . . . There are people in China who respect English writers and love the Russians too, but these people are incapable of knowing their own writers. Readers, by and large, are helpless creatures, unable to decide what or whom to read. Obviously, the choice must be made for them by the critics. Unfortunately, most of our criticism is nothing but a long series of advertisements by respective publishers. As a result, a book that sells must purport to be the best. The literary concepts of professors, of warriors even, and the weird tastes of readers—all these ravage the healthy sprouts of Chinese literature. Thus, promising writers are confined to one concept or another. . . .[3]

By 1929, purges within the Nationalist party were increasing. His business failure notwithstanding, Shen expressed his gratitude to the book merchants who had shown the least concern to writers. The situation was again desperate. More and more publishing houses had to close shop. It seemed that every magazine was "too radical" for the Nationalists' taste. *The Torrent* was gone. Creation Society magazines went out of business. Their editors were arrested. Even Lu Hsün who set himself up as a kind of puppet leader was threatened. Alone, he advocated revolutionary literature through *Sprouts Monthly,* edited by Yao P'eng-tzu, a fiction writer. Presumably because of the magazine's name and its almost comical editorials, Shen could not resist commenting that "they have isms, but not writing!"

Not so comic, however, was the fact that Shen, Hu, and Ting were at least a thousand dollars in debt. And all three were again without work.

CHAPTER 7

Bending with the Wind

BANKRUPTCY seemed inevitable. For the more versatile Shen, however, there was another option. With the assistance of Hu Shih, then President of Wu-sung Chinese Institute, the erstwhile publisher and editor began a new career as Instructor of Chinese Literature and writer-in-residence. It was the autumn of 1929, and with the change of season came subtle shifts in government policy and bureaucracy which did not suit Shen's former partners at all. Hu Yeh-p'in's radicalism, both in thought and writing, was now so thorough that few publishers would risk accepting his work. He and Ting Ling were forced to leave Shanghai and accept positions in a high school in Tsinan, Shantung. They began teaching at about the same time Shen assumed his duties with the Chinese Institute.

Once again, the three were living apart. This time, though, the separation deepened into a spiritual rift. From the beginning, Hu Yeh-p'in had structured his literary ambitions according to political ideology; consequently, art was often served but marginally. When finally it became apparent that Hu had failed in his efforts to promote proletarian literature, he turned to the Communist party for support. This made for a complete separation with Shen.

Early in 1926, Shen's ailing mother and youngest sister joined him in Peking. To support his family, Shen had to write a great deal on the side. In addition, he accepted a part-time job at Tsi-nan University in Shanghai, where he taught "The History of Chinese Fiction" two hours a week. In spite of the long hours and financial burden, Shen's writing was approaching its maturity. Wen Tzu-ch'uan, an essayist, wrote in his preface to a volume of *Selected Stories and Essays of Shen Ts'ung-wen* (1957):

I remember that summer (1929), in a small bookstore in front of Tsi-nan University, I bought a volume of short stories by Shen

Ts'ung-wen, entitled *An Honest Man*. A classmate, seeing this, said to me: "How could you have bought the work of this man! The sentences and syntax in his fiction are unintelligible. If you don't believe me, go ahead and read that collection; see if you can continue. . . ." Driven by curiosity, I bought all his collections, even tracked down those magazines where he was published. I wanted to read him systematically; my classmate's criticism I found unfair, unreasonable. I was thinking then that an editor might, out of carelessness, publish a story whose sentences were not always intelligible; but how could all magazine editors be *that* careless? I decided that it must have been my classmate's prejudice.[1]

Political divisiveness had also infiltrated the university, with many writers of the Crescent Moon Society holding teaching positions there. Shen was the youngest of them all. Although not officially enrolled in Shen's "History of Chinese Fiction," Wen Tzu-ch'uan frequently sat in:

God knows why I kept on attending his sessions. But after reading his work, I just had to see him in action, had to hear him speak. His notes were always well prepared, comprehensive, perhaps even comparable to Lu Hsün's *A Brief History of Chinese Fiction*, which was published later. From half a year's earnest attendance, I compiled huge volumes of notes. . . .
My overall impression of this country writer was his simplicity. Of medium height, neither too thin, nor heavy, he was almost habitually in a long gown of blue pique or linen, western trousers and black shoes, with a big cloth parcel in his hand. He was brisk, like a bill collector, or a barber out on an errand. On the bridge of his nose sat a pair of spectacles behind which peered big round eyes reflecting profound intelligence and a kind of serenity. When he spoke to you, a tranquil smile would now and then creep onto his face. At the time, he must have been twenty-eight or twenty-nine. . . .[2]

Not everybody was as impressed as Wen Tzu-ch'uan, however. While many of his students found Shen's classes absorbing, there were those who regarded the lecturer with envy and suspicion. In November, 1950, Ting Ling published "The Life of an Honest Man." Something of a revolutionary's almanac, it traced the personal and ideological differences between Shen Ts'ung-wen, Hu Yeh-p'in, and Ting Ling herself.

Fundamentally, Yeh-p'in is different from Shen Ts'ung-wen and me. Unlike me, who can be self-indulgent and fanciful, Yeh-p'in is a pragmatist always, never permitting himself, as does Shen Ts'ung-wen, to appease the upper-class. Yeh-p'in is firm, forever at odds with the rulers. From the very beginning, Shen Ts'ung-wen was enamored of the genteel, and this led to his affiliation with the Crescent Moon Society and the Modern Critic School. He was not content with the modest lot of a struggling writer; no, he had to become a professor; he had to teach at the Wu-sung Chinese Institute. Unconsciously, he was afraid of those who originated the Proletarian Literary Movement. . . .[3]

Such an assessment seems hardly fair. Indeed, when one is reminded of the shabby and brutalizing conditions surrounding Shen's development, it is harsh. Like Quixote, Hu Yeh-p'in and Ting Ling rode off to topple windmills; their quest, anchored as it was in proletarian literature, was always romantic. They had no one else to worry about but themselves. In a sense, they were more than husband and wife—they were brothers in spirit, comrades in arms. Their failures, therefore, were political ones, affecting not bone and sinew, but thought and theory. It was not for lack of idealism and dramaturgy that Shen failed to measure up to his friends' expectations. Since adolescence, he had worn filial obligation like a tail: concern for an ailing mother, care of a younger sister. No reasonably serious writer takes up potboiling for sheer diversion, and Shen knew, as critics and authors already knew, that he was better than that. Yeh-p'in and Ting Ling demanded nothing less than absolute dedication, perhaps the kind that took Gauguin to Tahiti and posterity, at the expense of home and family. In that respect at least, Shen was different from Hu and Ting, which did not mean that his dedication to art was of a lesser degree. Besides, teaching afforded an author an opportunity to reach a potential audience. After his final separation from Hu and Ting, Shen had no way to convey to them the internal conflict that trailed him to Wuhan University in Wu-chang, Hupeh, in the fall of 1930. There, teaching a three-hour course, he was free to face again an old nightmare:

When I went out, I met soldiers. I saw people shaving off pig-tails; I witnessed executions. Again I was dazed by the stupid, the

colorless, the commonplace. Again, the sounds which I thought I
had lost forever in the last ten years. Again, it seemed, I was one
more non-entity as I leaned against a wall or sidled with a crowd of
dirty faces to watch another foolish spectacle. To prove that I was
one of them, I acknowledged and returned their smiles. All this
while confronted with still bleeding heads . . . and musing on other
dirty heads still attached to their dirty necks.

Situations like this somehow nurtured me; my melancholy was
my amusement, too. There was nothing in the world I could not
appreciate; everything invigorated me . . . I seemed younger. . . .[4]

Once more, Shen was struck by how little had been accomplished in the way of social reform. Virtually nothing had been
done in Wu-chang to improve living conditions. A haphazard
life and lack of official concern for the populace caused him
to examine and identify his own roots. In his preface to *The
Border Town*, a short novel, he wrote: "I have an unutterable
warm love for peasants and soldiers. This feeling is everywhere,
in all my writings."[5]

Wu-chang was to make Shen, both as an individual and as a
writer. As a soldier, he had endured the typical elements of
Wu-chang in countless villages; he had heard the same screams,
seen the same blood, recorded the same barbarities. As a private
citizen, and still helpless, still steeped in anonymity, the best
he could do was to transform rural artifacts into prose—yeoman
fiction with a soldier's perspective but made lyrical by folk
sentiment. Grim but evocative testimonials of this period are
the stories, *Po-tzu, Hsiao-hsiao, The Husband, Kitchen Garden,
Lamp,* and *Black Night.*

On his spring vacation in Shanghai, 1931, Shen learned of
his father's death. He had seen the old man but twice in the past
twenty years. There was little joy in the conciliation with Hu
Yeh-p'in and Ting Ling, now the parents of a sixty-day-old son,
and barely subsisting. The luckless couple had made new and
powerful enemies; on January 17 of that year, the Nationalist
government arrested Yeh-p'in. A month later, Ting Ling received
word that her husband was dead. Shen Ts'ung-wen accompanied
the widow and her son to Hunan. Upon his return to Shanghai
in March, he found that he was too late for a reappointment at
Wuhan University. He had lost his job. Fortunately, he had

other work alternatives. From Peking, he received a letter from the poet Hsü Chih-mo: "If you are tired of Shanghai, come to Peking. While every post seems filled and the land is crawling with people, if you come there will be room for you. After all, how many ounces of rice a day can one man like you consume? Do not worry. The price of rice will not rise once you get to Peking."[6]

Shen's memories of Peking were not pleasant. But the jesting tone of the poet's letter was more than he could resist. By May, he was in Peking. Hsü Chih-mo was teaching at Peking University. In "Learning From Reality," an essay written in October, 1947, Shen summed up his feelings about his return to the city:

The peasant Shen Ts'ung-wen thought that in his three-year stay in Shanghai he had seen enough. Yet, here he was in Peking again, virtually an exile among 1,500,000 citizens. From this, I understand I had only accomplished the second leg of my journey and that another long and lonely phase was waiting for me. Yet, compared to the rank commercialism and plotting and politicking of Shanghai and Nanking, Peking's sunshine and northerly winds seemed almost inspirational, tempting me to climb a new peak, to be closer to nature—and to live.[7]

Now, Shen's literary style began to develop and change in a number of ways: by trying to catch the flavor and nuance of the provincial Hunan dialect, he began to develop a new style.

My work may be somewhat troublesome and dull when compared to others. I've tried to retain my simplicity, I have also learned from other writers. My work should be liberated from theories, even from traditional forms I have adopted in the past. Novel literary devices then, I expanded or rebuilt, constructing even newer concepts on which I built other foundations. Thus, I dug out historical legends; the stale, such as fables and Buddhist disciplines, I rearranged in a new lyrical way. Rhymed prose and Buddhist enigmas, I tried to break up and then combine with slang and idiom to achieve a new effect. This effect I tried to link with geographical scenes and human relationships. With this in mind, I traveled back and forth between Ch'in-chou in Manchuria and Wuhan, then to Tsingtao for three years.[8]

For the next two years, the young instructor taught at Tsingtao University. The experience was part sojourn, part incarceration. Blue sky, scenic coastlines, lapping sea waves—and dead bodies washed ashore. The tide brought in seashells white as ivory or dark as jade. But, however calm the landscape, there always seemed to be a reminder of political regimes, something ominous in the air. Within ten months, Shen lost five more friends. One of these was Hsü Chih-mo who died in a plane crash in Tsi-nan. In *Random Talks on Hsü Chih-mo,* Liang Shih-ch'iu wrote: "Shen Ts'ung-wen had always been favored by Hsü Chih-mo. It was during the latter's editorship of the Peking *Morning Post* from 1925 to 1926 that Shen published many of his early works. This extended to the Shanghai *Crescent Moon Monthly* which published Shen's work upon Chih-mo's recommendation . . ."[9]

More about Hsü Chih-mo is to be found in Shen's preface to a revised volume of short stories, *Ah-Chin*: "Were it not for Hsü Chih-mo, I would have become a policeman, or I would have simply deteriorated in Peking under somebody's thatched roof. When you, dear reader, have finished this book, I hope that you will pay due homage to our poet, departed too early and from whom I received a torch. The warmth you find here is his originally."[10]

Bachelorhood ended for Shen in 1933 when he married one of his students, Chang Chao-ho, after a long courtship. At this time, Shen also completed a series of short stories adapted from Buddhist classics and dedicated to his little brother-in-law; the book saw publication the following year, when its author became editor of the literary supplement of *Ta-kung Pao* in Tientsin. His first son, Lung-lung, was born in 1934. After a brief visit to Hunan, Shen wrote his famous short novel, *The Border Town.*

Since September 18, 1931, Japanese aggression had been felt in Manchuria. The initial invasion was referred to as the Mukden Incident. It caused some unease but no great alarm. However, on February 1, 1932, Japanese gunboats bombarded Nanking in earnest. Then, barely a year later, the Japanese struck again, this time in Jehol, north of Peking, penetrating westward through Inner Mongolia and southward into the northeastern provinces of China including Peking and the great port of Tientsin. T. Mende described the invasion: "In the East, Japan was creeping along the border of Siberia.... Daily, her planes had been circling over China's cities, flying low to intimidate the population with the bombs visible in their racks. Japanese troops were scattered all over North China."[11]

After controlling Northeast China through a puppet state (Manchoukuo, "Empire of Manchuria"), Japan's next step was to establish a so-called North China Political Council so that the Japanese forces could exert further pressure on China. Shen, now writer-editor-educator, was moved to comment in "Learning From Reality":

> After the Northeastern territories had fallen into Japanese hands, enemy forces closed in upon us. Peking, Tientsin, and North China had a tendency to change. For the sake of our country's future, everything had to be rebuilt in the Northwest, Honan and Shantung, no matter how trivial the problem was. With the central government completely withdrawn from North China, the only weapon left was literature with its power to resist a strong neighbor. The over-thirty generation had left us nothing but stereotypes. But there would still be the children, our youth—they had to be instilled with some kind of national pride and courage. To this end, some friends and a few teachers accepted a consignment from an organization related to National Defense to edit and print fundamental readings for students....[12]

The project which started with the publication of primary school readers had appreciable effect. To facilitate what in reality was nationalistic propaganda, even school functionaries had to resign from their jobs. Rank and file were required to make sacrifices. A university president resigned his office to assume the less glamorous role of pamphlet distributor. Shen himself willingly tackled menial tasks. With him, a famous professor and department head at the university joined in the work.

In 1936, Shen's work was temporarily interrupted when his wife had her second child, a boy, Hu-hu. The Sino-Japanese War, which finally broke out on July 7, 1937, shattered the plans that Shen and his friends had made to establish a new literature for the young. Wordlessly, they sat around a fireplace, burned their campaign literature, and separately left Peking. For four dreary months, Shen lived in a municipal city on the River Yüan.

When Wuhan was bombarded by the Japanese, Shen evacuated his family to Kunming, where he found a teaching post at the Southwest Associated University. In April, 1940, he was made editor of *Chan-kuo-ts'e*.

Kunming was a hothouse, a midden shed, of burnt-out intellectuals. They lived by their wits, harassed by poverty and inflation. Nobody paid attention to them; they fell sick, died, and were unmourned. Shen's magazine folded in 1941. He wrote of that dismal episode: "This is the fourth leg in the Countryman's journey ... rather long, rather lonely, rather difficult ... but I accepted the situation in much the same manner I did when I first came to Peking...."[13]

During this period of his life, he wrote very little. From 1938 to 1940, his published work included only a volume of essays, *West of Hunan*, and *Long River*, a novel which, when it was serialized in a Hong Kong newspaper, had been considerably shortened. Censorship had caught up with Shen.

The Sino-Japanese War ended in August, 1945, but only after both nations had become involved in World War II. The summer of 1946 found Shen Ts'ung-wen in Peking—"The city which I had known for twenty-five years and left for nine." His creative powers were renewed and he had a rewarding job at Peking University. The war was behind him now, but he was faced with a new, more difficult struggle, against the power of the censors.

CHAPTER 8

A Critique (I):
Characters in Shen Ts'ung-wen's Fiction

IN his preface to *Alice in China*, Shen Ts'ung-wen stated that he could elicit fifty different associations from a single root source. This is not as presumptuous as it may sound. The best of Shen Ts'ung-wen's fiction renders a prismatic effect, perhaps not visibly, and perhaps not technically, but symbolically. Then, too, there is that broad expanse of literary forms wherein he could experiment, grow, and en route, transmit to a fast awakening Chinese public the beginnings of ethnic pride. Shen Ts'ung-wen is credited with having authored no less than fifty volumes of published works which include poetry, short stories, novels, articles, fables, biographies, travelogues, plays and critical essays. Such an all-encompassing authorial view naturally requires an equally panoramic view of mankind. This has been ably demonstrated in Shen Ts'ung-wen's writings by *dramatis personae* portrayed in all walks of life: clerks, professors, young people, politicians, landlords, writers, bureaucrats, bandits, boatmen, concubines, prostitutes, laborers, traders, smugglers, shopkeepers, hunters, and so forth. Each of these characters is held up for scrutiny, never for ridicule or condemnation.

Behind every versatility in the arts lies a specific genre; each practicing artist has his own special focus, a subject or a field in which his vision and particular talent are ideally matched. Shen Ts'ung-wen's field may be called Countryman—people who work the land, people who live on the waters.

I am a Countryman. The statement is neither pompous nor self-effacing. The countryman is one whose personality is deeply rooted in the country. He has his own sense of love, hatred, sorrow and happiness. As opposed to the city man, the countryman is conservative and stubborn, lacking guile, but not alertness. His love for the soil is consummate. He is serious about everything, so much so that he appears almost idiotic.[1]

The above passage from *Exercise*, an essay, carries with it Shen Ts'ung-wen's definition of just what a countryman is or should be.

Random Sketches on a Trip to West Hunan is a minor classic that etches Shen Ts'ung-wen's Countryman in detail:

Here is a group of Countrymen who know how to enjoy themselves—hunters, fishermen and laborers braiding bamboo strands. If my guess is right, the one sitting beside me, his hands stretched to the fire, a sparkling thimble on his middle finger, is a country tailor. All of them, on the Dragon-boat Festival each year, will be down by the river for the rowing. For the rest of the year, they are right here, partaking of a simple life. To this small restaurant they will come to watch those boats with hoisted sails and flexing oars, moving to and fro, the sunset, the water-birds, whatever. They suffer from domestic loss or a neighbor's enmity; but no misfortune is overwhelming enough to disrupt the harmony they share with nature. They live by the code of nature, with all the other entities, living or inanimate, which radiate or dissolve with the changing of the seasons, and follow the rising and setting of sun and moon.[2]

In much of Shen Ts'ung-wen's fiction, the elements constitute Supreme Law: his characters, thriving or obscure, very often have no substantial existence beyond nature's boundaries; for they are creatures who must of necessity live in harmony with the elements. Therein lies their passion, their obstinacy—their insistence on their own code within a cycle which may be both friend and foe. By extension, it is principally with such an orthodoxy, subconscious though it may be, yet also cultivated, that Shen Ts'ung-wen the vagabond ripened and matured as Shen Ts'ung-wen, the venerable Chinese author. It is to his credit too, that he did not neglect the darker side of his world. His fiction is infected, as reality must unavoidably be, with the vile and the vicious. Even the Countryman does not escape the taint of humanity: he is both affectionate and unlovable, young and senile, pure and covetous. By turns, the Countryman is a minority, perishable and misunderstood. He is, in short, civilization's lonely bastard born out of culturelock between progress and passivity.

To some extent, Shen Ts'ung-wen's Countryman is the cousin of Camus' Stranger. Both are alienated. The Stranger exists in a godless society without values; the Countryman lives in a world ravaged by civilization. Both rely on sensations. They must touch and see and hear and smell. Beyond their senses, neither expects much from life—except death. The parallel ends there, however. The Stranger rebels against and is contemptuous of death: the Countryman accepts its inevitability— he lives with death, and is at peace with it. Both the Stranger and the Countryman have no future, no hope, no illusions, and yet, oddly, go on and on because there is nothing else, and it is, however vaguely, still good to live. In the final analysis, both Stranger and Countryman are absurd.

Although Shen Ts'ung-wen's characters represent every sort of human condition, our critique of his fiction will focus specifically on his Countryman; the absurd Countryman dislocated in time and space; the alienated Countryman, ill-used by modern civilization; the Countryman distorted by war and revolution; the ideal Countryman; the Countryman in contrast to the City-man. This critique will also focus on Shen Ts'ung-wen's short fiction, since his main contribution to Chinese letters is the short story.

I *Three Men and a Girl*

A grisly incident Shen Ts'ung-wen describes in his autobiography (see Chapter 2) was to be lifted, almost intact, from its source to flesh out the author's morbid but absorbing short story *Three Men and A Girl*. The autobiographical incident concerns a young beancurd shopkeeper who desecrates the grave of a young girl the very night of her burial. In the secrecy of a stone cave not far from the grave, the grave robber sleeps with her body. Three days later, he returns the dead girl to her grave.

Following is a version of the incident from the short story: An Army battalion march in the rain to a new post. They are stationed at a desolate family temple. When they arrive, the

bugler climbs the stone lion to blow a martial response. Two big
white dogs come from the end of the street. A girl's voice calls
them back. The dogs turn and run away. The bugler, after an accidental fall from the stone lion, is crippled. In the company of
another soldier (the narrator of the story) he frequents a beancurd shop to watch its owner at work. These visits become more
interesting when the two soldiers encounter the two big white
dogs and, from a distance, their mistress, a pretty young girl. The
two soldiers try their best to win the trust of the dogs. When
the soldiers are stupid, or behave badly toward the dogs, the
young shopkeeper merely smiles. Even when the soldiers taunt
the shopkeeper, he smiles. Six months pass without incident. The
two soldiers have now befriended the dogs, but are no closer
to the girl. And neither can elicit any response from the smiling
young shopkeeper. One day, news reaches them that the girl
has killed herself by swallowing gold pieces. The bugler disappears from the temple, returns to tell the other soldier that
he has been grave hunting. Someone else got to the grave ahead
of him, however, because the girl's body is gone. Then, the
soldiers learn that the shopkeeper has disappeared. They later
learn that the body of the girl was discovered in a stone cave.

The honorable young beancurd shopkeeper is Shen Ts'ung-
wen's absurd Countryman. The difference between the biographical incident and the short story is that there are two additional
characters in the short story. Why does the author add two
characters? How does he depict the absurd Countryman? The
story begins with this passage:

Nobody knew why it should rain when the army marched to a
new post.
We didn't know. Maybe the men who were in charge of military
necessities knew—when it rained, or was muddy, there would be
more demand for the straw shoes for the soldiers who had to walk
in the rain. They might gain something from it. We didn't know. It
was always complicated. Even the regimental commander didn't
know, because he wore leather boots. Every time we started out,
there was always the rain.[3]

The story's beginning, full of absurdity and boredom, recalls
Camus' *The Stranger*. It is a reminder of the unpredictability
of nature. The reader is first introduced to the young bugler:

The bugler climbed the stone lion, one hand holding onto the statue lit by the setting sun, the other clutching a bugle of purple brass. He blew a martial response, the sound floating in the evening wind, pleasurable and haunting. The sky was embered with sun, white smoke billowed from chimneys, and drifted like waves to other roofs. Young women in bleached, newly washed, moon-blue clothes and embroidered aprons, babies in their arms, stood under the eaves, gazing into the distance.[4]

Character deterioration is deftly handled in the person of the bugler who, after his accidental fall from the stone lion, is crippled for life. In rapid progression, the bugler turned patient sinks beyond redemption, physically, spiritually, morally. At this point, the author turns his attention to the dogs:

We tried our best to win the trust of the two dogs by spending our money on feed. At first, as if the two beasts knew our intentions concerning their mistress, they would sniff at the feed and turn away. Later, when the shopkeeper threw the feed to them, they would look at him understandingly and eat it, as if they knew it was not poison. . . .[5]

In time, the two dogs became friendlier. Upon seeing us, they would come over, though cautiously, to the beancurd shop. We hated these beasts, yet liked them, too. Even if we were getting along nicely, they would leave us when they heard the girl's voice calling from across the street.[6]

As straight narrative, these passages are informative on the realistic level; they add an extra dimension of psychological undertone implicit in the relationship between the three men and the dogs, which are ambivalent symbols: they represent both the cruelty of death and its attraction. (They function as symbols—symbolism in general in the story will be discussed later in the book.) The two soldiers hate the dogs as only men can hate the image of death. Still, the dogs' owner is coveted in whatever dreams the two soldiers entertain secretly, and for this reason they cannot help but show some affection for the beasts. Only the young beancurd shopkeeper seems favored in this strange group. He is, as it develops, the real friend of death, represented by the dogs.

Who is this shopkeeper? What is he like?

The beancurd shopkeeper was a young man, strong and reticent. Happy in his everyday work, he did business with everyone. . . . We only knew that he had moved here from the country. Once in a while, some of his relatives would visit him at his shop. From this we gathered that the man did not come from a poor family. His business was flourishing; and, as he told me, he sent home all his earnings. Asked whether he was planning on getting married, he only smiled. He knew quite a few songs and had a very pleasant singing voice, better than any we heard in our battalion. He played checkers, and even though he couldn't read, he could recognize a few words: chariot, minister, and guard. Needing no account books for his trade, he relied on his memory for the tallying of debts and credits. He took us for friends; he was neither wary nor servile. . . . My friend and I often talked with him in the beancurd shop. We talked about the girl across the street. Sometimes, the bugler and I were stupid, coarse in our behavior, or we acted abominably toward those two dogs. The young shopkeeper merely smiled. Although we could never detect any sign of ridicule in his smile, it nevertheless seemed some mystery lay behind it.

I said, "What are you smiling at? Don't you think she's a beauty? Won't you admit that those two dogs have better luck than we?" As usual, words had no discernible effect on him. His only response was that sincere, bashful smile.

"Why do you smile? You Countrymen . . . totally without any understanding of beauty! You must like your women with big boobs and bigger hips. You must like swine, cattle—because they are meaty and big enough to suit you! But this is only because you can't distinguish beauty!"

Sometimes the crippled bugler would say in exasperation, "Son of a bitch—damned lucky dogs!"

To taunt the shopkeeper, my friend asked if he was willing to become a dog for a chance to be near the girl every day. As was his wont at such delicate moments, he only blushed and pushed particularly hard at the grinding stone—still smiling.[7]

These passages, perhaps more than any others in the story, demonstrate Shen Ts'ung-wen's skill in characterization. The two soldiers are used as stage accessories, or secondary lights, to enhance the frontispiece, the beancurd shopkeeper with his "idiotic" smile. In the eyes of the soldiers, this smile is the smile of a Countryman, and is therefore worthy of contempt. The smile is enigmatic, a fixture, the only relief in what purports to be a mask of inscrutability, not only of the beancurd shopkeeper, but of an entire social class. When the two soldiers taunt the shopkeeper by dragging him to see the corpses of criminals, he grins at the cadavers, too. This smile, the author seems to say, is both weapon and sanctuary for the young Countryman who can look at death without fear. This smile links him with death. It also links him with the girl.

The girl came out of the door and stood there; the two big white dogs bounded up and down by her side, circling around her, licking her small hands with their darting red tongues.

We stopped talking. The three of us were looking at her. The girl appeared to notice the bruises on the faces of the bugler and me, which had come from the fight. She smiled, with no suggestion of fear or suspicion.[8]

The Countryman and the girl wear the same mask—the smile of the innocent. Moreover, they are symbolically virgins in a land violated by soldiers. The girl, vibrant and unattainable, is associated with, is, perhaps, a personification of, death. Since the soldiers cannot get closer to the girl, malaise sets in. They call each other names, get into a fistfight. Moral and physical decrepitude (the bugler's) clash with an inferiority complex and impotence (the narrator's). Wedged in the middle, the indestructible shopkeeper wards off bigotry and violence with his impenetrable smile.

Thus far in the story, the Countryman has not directly spoken a word. He has been depicted from the narrator-soldier's point of view. It is as if the author has deliberately inserted a layer of glass between the Countryman and the reader. Where no voice is heard, no recognizable intelligence is implied, and the reader is left with nothing but a transparency. This technique intensifies the atmosphere of the absurd—a literary device similarly employed by Camus to portray his Stranger.

Fittingly, the girl's suicide (she swallows several gold pieces) is also absurd. The suicide is abrupt, with no explanation or justification from the author. The death of their loved one affects the three men in diverse ways. A deep melancholy assails the crippled bugler. More philosophically inclined, the squad-leader, the narrator, arrives at his own peculiar rationale for the girl's death: since the flower vase (the girl) never really belonged to him, its having been broken should not distress him. The young Countryman does not look as cheerful as he did before, but he shows no other sign of emotion. At this juncture, the story withdraws from the absurd and advances into the metaphysical realm. The bugler disappears from the temple and returns, looking grimy and shaken. The village superstition he repeats has an ominous overtone: a girl who perishes from swallowing gold pieces may be resurrected within seven days of her death by the embrace of a man. The bugler has gone grave hunting two days after the girl has been buried, hoping to fulfill the prophecy. The girl's body, however, is gone. Now, the three male protagonists offer three separate points of view: the bugler and his cripple's love for the girl; the narrator and his vulgarian's covetousness; the shopkeeper, the natural man, and his affinity with the young girl. Because he is the natural man, it is right, according to Shen, that the shopkeeper should leave no imprint on a civilization represented by the likes of the crippled bugler and the empty shell of a squad leader. Shen Ts'ung-wen offers but minimal description of the Countryman; yet the essence of his character is clear: his inscrutable smile, his spiritual link with the girl. What the author has given us is aura, not outline; secondary characters surmise but do not fully participate in the tragedy. Indirectly, through atmospheric enhancement, Shen Ts'ung-wen has fashioned a fable around the nonentity of his Countryman—nonentity, however, only insofar as his invisible social values are concerned. *Three Men and a Girl* states with quiet grace and passion that we call the "stranger" in our midst an "idiot" at our own peril. When the Countryman disappears and the girl's body is discovered in a stone cave half a mile from the grave, there is nothing more disturbing than the notion of a once invisible man revealing to us at last a vision of his disembodied face.

II *Construction*

In the teahouse of a small town by the river, the owner of a second-hand shop and a retired soldier are talking mysteriously about some business to be transacted the evening of the following day. At the next table, a worker and a soldier stationed in town are listening to the conversation. The worker does not understand any of the talk. The soldier, on the other hand, gathers that the two men are talking about the illegal sale of guns one of them will steal somewhere. The soldier tells the worker he wants to rob the gun smuggler of the money he will earn from the illegal sale. The worker hesitates at the suggestion. The soldier laughs at him. Finally, the worker swears that he will participate in the crime. The next day, while carrying a load of timber for the construction of a school building financed by a foreign missionary organization, the worker is so preoccupied with thoughts of the planned robbery that he cuts his left hand on a log. He begins to bleed and his blood stains the timber. In the evening, the worker and the soldier return to the teahouse. The gun smuggler has not succeeded in obtaining the guns. The worker leaves to walk along the river. While urinating under a tree in the dark, he hears someone coming. It is the priest sponsored by the missionary organization, sent out to preach to the workers on the construction project. The priest thinks that the worker is drunk and wants to take him home. The worker refuses. The priest tries to detain the man, and in so doing, feels the small hammer the worker has carried for the robbery of the gun smuggler. The priest accuses the worker of carrying a weapon and grabs at the wounded left hand. The worker hits the priest on the head with the hammer.

The worker who kills a priest without any apparent reason is a Countryman, dislocated and alienated by modern civilization. Shen Ts'ung-wen's tragic vision of the social status of modern China is embodied in the worker on two levels: firstly, the external, or realistic level; and secondly, the internal, or inner consciousness, a psychological level.

Of rural origins, this man was a worker employed by the Construction Company for thirty cents a day. Punctually every morning, he came out of the shabby lodgings made of boards and went to work in the mud. Later, he lunched on coarse rice. He was a reliable and useful worker, a foolish but honest man, a creature worthy of being cheated by the foreign priest and fooled into laboring forever in the name of God.[9]

This foolish but honest Countryman is obtrusive in a world where "all manpower is mobilized for one clever engineer's plan." The language of such a world is foreign to him:

"I didn't know what they were talking about."
"About boxes."
"Boxes?"
"Cases."
"What are boxes and cases?"
"That thing I have. Understand?"
"Oh, I see. . . ."[10]

The Countryman here is a physical presence only; the description pertaining to him is plain and direct. The soldier's scornful laughter goads him into complicity, however, and we are given insight into the workings of his mind:

He warmed himself under the worn-out quilt in his squalid and stinking room, and he went to sleep. *He dreamed of fighting and beating someone and taking away from him coins worth about eight dollars.* At the moment he came into possession of the coins, he woke up. He went out and pissed in the chilly moonlight. . . .[11] (italics mine)

Contrasted with what is going on in the mind of the worker is Shen Ts'ung-wen's portrait of the dehumanized world in which the worker must live. "When the sunlight shone on the faces of the workers, they looked even more inhuman. . . . It was hard to find one reasonably attractive face among the 300 present. . . ."[12] The foreman calls the workers by numbers and treats them as thieves. When they are bored, they entertain themselves by pitching stones at a cigarette box in a ditch. In such an oppressive atmosphere, it is hardly surprising that while hauling timber for the construction of the school, the worker becomes obsessed by the plans he has made to rob the gun smugglers. As the story progresses to its inevitable conclusion, the author cues the reader every step of the way.

He was thinking of it while loading the timber and pushing carts full of it along Riverside Street. Children called him Idiot. He didn't seem to hear them. . . . *His left hand was cut by the timber he was carrying. It began to bleed.* The man only uttered a faint curse, "Damn it." He wiped his hand on the leg of his dirty, worn-out blue trousers. They were stained with blood and turned black. He picked up a handful of mud and covered his wound with it. . . .[13]

Very simply, but poignantly, Shen Ts'ung-wen's language bares the worker's mind to the reader. It is the mind of a natural man who believes in, and occasionally even resembles, mud from the earth, so that he may, at times, appear in the eyes of others an idiot. On another level, however, Shen's language demonstrates a vision of modern China: the Countryman, wounded by modern civilization (industry, technology, Christianity, and education), which is symbolized by the construction of the school by a foreign missionary organization, may only be cured by mud from his native soil. This vision is emphasized again and again, and in a variety of situations.

The dwarf, finding the countryman smiling at him, became even more excited.

He said, "Brother, I am sorry for your hand, wounded for such unimportant matters. Have you ever killed a tiger? Have you ever caught a porcupine? Have you ever climbed a tree? Have you ever held the waist of a woman? . . ."[14]

This is the author's conception of the natural man dislocated by industrial society. The implication is that natural man, if he is to be injured, must only be injured by the toil necessary to survive in the natural world—for instance, the killing of a tiger. Ironically, however, the worker's hand has been injured as the result of an industrial accident.

The Countryman was hauling timber up the slope. In spite of his wound, his left hand persisted in its task. *The blood oozing through the mud covering the wound stained the timber....* The dwarf warned him that he shouldn't let the timber be stained by blood since his load was to be used for the roof of the auditorium of the school.[15] (italics mine)

This passage, of course, is highly symbolic: modern China (represented by the new school) owes its existence to the blood of its Countrymen. Significantly, it is only when the worker learns that the gun smugglers have failed to steal the guns that

he feels the pain of his wound. After leaving the teahouse, he
hears the sounds made by gamblers and wants to gamble, too.
He puts his hand into his trouser's pocket and touches the
small hammer he has carried for the robbery. The hammer reminds him of all that he has dreamt about the robbery. "He
felt like making some trouble that evening."[16] It is one of the
absurd, but pivotal, moments many of Shen Ts'ung-wen's
ill-used characters cannot seem to shake off. It is that latent,
dark force, so persistent that it will not rest until sated.

The worker was walking along the river. The weather was good
for thinking, and his thoughts wandered. He thought that he might
come to meet the gun smuggler, or somebody else, who would carry
silver dollars and golden rings, at which time he would lift up the
small hammer with his good hand, hit him on the head, or anywhere
else, and get something unexpected. He had never had a similar
thought before. . . .[17]

Shen Ts'ung-wen explores the inner consciousness of the
Countryman before propelling him to his doom, the murder of
the priest. The story does not end with the priest's death, however. Even when he is lying dead at his feet, the worker doesn't
understand. He goes back to work as usual. He feels nothing
for his crime. The next evening, his soldier friend takes him to
visit a prostitute. When the soldier puts his friend's hand on the
woman's arm, she senses the violent, ungovernable force in him.
He is, as the soldier says, "a tiger fresh from the mountains;
everything is so strange to him that he is frightened."[18]

A year later, the missionary organization decides to set up a
monument in memory of the priest. Among others, the worker
is sent to dig the ground for the foundation of the monument.
He works so hard that he is given a bonus. He returns to the
prostitute, a woman with fat hips and big feet. He spends the
night with her.

Ho Yü-po, a leftist critic of the thirties, wrote in *Criticisms of
Modern Chinese Writers*, "Most of Shen Ts'ung-wen's works
are empty; there is nothing but shards of pictures and insigni-
cant records of life. There is no vision at all. . . ."[19] On the
surface of Shen Ts'ung-wen's works, there seems to be nothing
but "shards of pictures and insignificant records of life"—the

trivialities of life. But Shen Ts'ung-wen's surface reality fairly
trembles with internal resonances, buried there to evoke his
vision of the human condition. In *Construction,* he writes about
a Countryman, ill-used by modern civilization. The story might
have ended with the death of the priest, and with the dark
images of the Countryman hovering over the body. But the
author's portrait of the Countryman is not complete until he has
shown him in light of the "shards of pictures and insignificant
records of life" that attest to the primitive innocence of the
human heart. The Countryman's first and second encounter with
the prostitute, the ensuing horseplay, the bonus he receives for
his work on the monument—these are superb final touches, and
further proof that Shen Ts'ung-wen excels not only as an artist
but as a humanist as well—one whose commitment to modern
China is complete.

Construction, its accomplishments notwithstanding, is one
of Shen Ts'ung-wen's stories that suffers a structural deficiency.
The description of the worker's life is random and much too
long; the author's comments about the workers, soldiers, the
rich and the poor, are intrusive. These excesses detract from the
story's central purpose which is to illuminate the primitive about
the character of an ill-used Countryman.

III *Hui Ming*

Hui Ming is an army cook whose company has been fighting
warlords in China. Hui Ming's small triangular army flag, one
that he wears wrapped around his waist, is his only memento of
ten years of fighting. It is his fervent hope that one day he will
"fly the flag at that place," a forest somewhere on the Chinese
frontier, where the army will tame the wilderness, produce food,
and fend for the country. He had gotten the idea from a speech
made by an army general some ten years previous. The general
had said, "Be brave! Fly your flag at that place." Now Hui
Ming's company is once again fighting warlords. For three days
nothing has happened. Hui Ming does not like the inactivity
because the corpses of soldiers will begin to rot and stink should
the fighting extend over the summer. Also, increasing the tempo
of battle may bring him closer to the dreamed-of forest where

he can fly his flag. But nothing happens. Hui Ming obtains a
chicken from villagers who have returned from the mountains
where they fled for shelter from the warring troops. Each day,
the chicken lays an egg. Eventually, twenty chicks are hatched.
The cook is so excited by this new development that he forgets
his surroundings. He tends to and enjoys the chicks as a mother
would her children, and as his love for the chicks intensifies,
so does his distaste for war. He is very happy to hear news
that the warlord chief who originally declared war has made
peace. It seems that he may never be allowed to fly his flag
in the frontier forest, but he is happy with his chickens. When
summer comes, there is not a single rotted corpse to spoil the
fresh air.

Hui Ming is one of Shen Ts'ung-wen's best efforts, and Hui
Ming is one of his best-drawn characters. He, again, is a Countryman, a natural man uprooted by revolution and war.

He had been a farmer. After the revolution against the emperor,
he had become an army cook in the Army of the Republic. . . .

He was four feet eight inches tall, with *long arms, long legs, a*
long face with a heavy nose that seemed heavier even than his
person, and a beard that should have grown *wild like weeds,* but
that was *trimmed short,* with the *stubble growing* horizontally
rather than vertically over his cheeks. . . .[20] (italics mine)

Like a hunter following the scent of prey, Shen Ts'ung-wen
tracks his pet archetype, and once again we are presented with
the embodiment of primitivism. Each descriptive word is carefully, meticulously chosen. Collectively, the words are a paean
to the Countryman's whole being: those pertaining to his body
suggest animal energy—those pertaining to his face suggest the
primeval earth with its natural properties inhibited in their
attempt to develop. This Countryman, too, is a stranger, a
stranger in a world of revolution and war. Even so, he is a man
whose faith in nature is strong:

He ignored all the teasing. What he saw was a huge forest, where
there would be no taunting military attorney, no handsome lieutenant,
no medals, no money, no jesting, no meanness. The forest, to him,
was the Chinese frontier, a foreign land, where the army would

be stationed to defend the country, to accomplish great things, settling the wilderness and producing bountiful harvests.

Here, there would be New Year's day, festivals, abundant food and tobacco, sentries and fighting. But it wouldn't be like what army life was like now. When would this dream be realized, and how? When asked this question, he could give no answer. And why was this dream more meaningful than promotion or wealth? He couldn't answer that question either. He only remembered what the general had said: "Fly your flag from the castle." He did have an army flag which he'd kept in the belief that someday soon it would be of use to him. When the time came, he would do what he had been told.[21]

Of *Hui Ming*, C. T. Hsia wrote in *A History of Modern Chinese Fiction*, "He (Shen) ascribes to the romantic and Taoist view that without a highly developed intellect and emotional capacity, one may nevertheless attain instinctive happiness and unconscious wisdom."[22] Hui Ming's instinctive happiness and unconscious wisdom do not ascribe to the Taoist, but to the Countryman. The Taoist is aloof from the world; the Countryman *lives* in the world, although his homeland is nature. He derives happiness from sensations, and unconscious wisdom from experience. He is realistic and earthbound, while the Taoist is not. "It is not for compassion for mankind, or the unity of any party, but for the bonus, that he rushes forward to fight."[23] He is so experienced in war that he can almost anticipate its development.

He was but a cook on the front. Yet, he was just as equipped for the war as any other soldier. He had already woven three pairs of straw shoes, had procured rope, several metal rice bowls, some tobacco, and fire tongs which he had bought at a high price from a firewood seller. He was sure that war, that sensational event, was not long in coming. When he watched the carts heavily loaded with arms and ammunition passing by with the wheels making deep ruts in the mud, he would laugh and shout. The horses, he said, were no good; when he had been marching to the front, he had carried a load of more than a hundred and twenty kilograms on his shoulders, while singing, and had talked in a loud, strong voice whenever he had stopped to rest.[24]

He relishes the sensations of war, the weariness, the thirst, the excitement, the disorder, the panic, the boredom. He is so

preoccupied with the war that he often wakens in the night
to the sound of imaginary guns firing. War prepares him for
adversity, and for adventure. War is the stink of corpses rotting
on the battlefield, the unwelcome prospect of fighting in the
summertime. The one bright spot in the world of darkness and
death is the dream of the forest on the frontier where the army
flag may one day fly. Hui Ming abandons even this vision, however, when the chicks are hatched. "The chickens came out of
their thin shells into the sunlight, chirping, with tender yellow
feathers. The sound drove Hui Ming crazy with joy...."[25]
C. T. Hsia sees "the affirmation of simple Taoist virtues in
the cook's spontaneous affection for, and joy over, the chickens."[26]
But it is the Countryman's sense of life, not Taoist virtue, that
drives Hui Ming crazy with joy over the chickens. The Countryman is too realistic and sensuous to be a Taoist.

When he returned to base, he was still a cook. When there was
no war, it seemed to him that he was farther away than ever from
the great forest with the army flag flying in the wind. He had the
chickens to take care of. And the tobacco left would see him through
another forty days. He was lucky. The month of June came and there
were no rotting corpses in the company. Hui Ming smiled at the
survivors. No one understood why.[27]

It is Hui Ming's smile, finally, that identifies him as another
of Shen Ts'ung-wen's Countrymen, the same smile that illumi-
nated the character of the beancurd vendor in *Three Men and
a Girl*, the smile of the innocent. A Countryman who, in spite
of war, is able to smile is one who will survive.

IV *The New and the Old*

The New and the Old is a two-part story about an executioner. Each part of the story—"The Ch'ing Dynasty," and "The
Republic"—treats of one event: the execution of criminals. In
the beginning of Part One, the character of the executioner
is a skillful young craftsman; later, he is an old, forgotten man.
His personal reactions to his work do not change from one part
of the story, or from one part of his life, to the next, but the
reactions of others to him as an executioner do change.

The Ch'ing Dynasty: Yang Chin-piao, the most skillful young executioner in a frontier town, is ordered to execute a criminal. He does his job skillfully and with dispatch. The moment the victim's head drops to the ground, the executioner runs to the Temple of the City God, prostrates himself before the god's image, and hides himself under a table. When the magistrate arrives, he pretends shock when he hears that someone has been murdered and that the murderer is at large. The executioner comes out from under the table to confess his crime. The magistrate who issued the execution order feigns anger at the killing and orders that the killer be severely punished. The executioner is beaten, then awarded a bonus for having done his job so well.

The Republic: The executioner is now an old man. The Imperial Dynasty has become the Republic of China. The number of executions have increased to such an extent that the government has been forced to have them performed by guns, which makes the aged executioner's skills obsolete. He is recompensed with another job, that of watching over the City Gate. One day, government officials order him to execute a man and a woman with his old saber. Afterward, he runs again to the Temple of the City God, falls on his knees, and hides under the table. The worshippers in the Temple mistake the old man with the bloody saber for a murderer or a lunatic. They try to catch him. Soldiers shoot at him. When, after some time, he is captured, he is insulted and mistreated. The executioner's latest victims, we learn, were Communists, and the military authorities wanted to make examples of them by having them executed in the old-fashioned way. Through it all, the hapless old executioner does not understand the whys or wherefores of his role. Fittingly, he comes to be known as "The Last Executioner."

The story gains its dramatic effect in the shift of time, from the past, to the present, from people's changing reactions to the executioner, and from the changes the executioner himself endures. Ironically, the action and reaction of the executioner's character do not change.

From The Ch'ing Dynasty:

The executioner ran to the Temple of the City God, knelt before the god, and hastily went under the incense table. He waited quietly.

In a little while, the magistrate came, with his servants beating gongs ahead of him. After burning incense to the god, the magistrate saw a man run up, fall on his knees, and heard him say, "A civilian has been killed outside the city limits. His head was severed. The place is bloody. The killer is at large."

The magistrate, who had issued the execution order and signed it with his own red ink, pretended shock and innocence. "Did this happen in broad daylight?" he asked.

He ordered men to find the killer and to arrest him. He also ordered that preparations be made for the killer's interrogation. Thinking that the magistrate was now prepared for his appearance, the executioner crept out from under the table and threw himself at the magistrate's feet. First, he identified himself. Then, he confessed that he had killed the man in question, and that he had the bloody saber as evidence.

The magistrate went through the motions of an interrogation. The executioner explained why he performed the execution, and begged for clemency. Finally, the magistrate shouted, "Punish the fool with forty lashes!" When the whipping had been accomplished, another subject handed the magistrate a small black pack, which the magistrate threw at the executioner. This was his bonus. . . .[28]

And, from The Republic:

He stepped up to the criminals. With two quick strokes of the saber, two heads fell to the ground. Upon seeing the spurting blood, he remembered what he had done thirty years ago. He began to run without looking back. He ran to the Temple of the City God where many women worshippers were burning incense, praying, and shaking the tube holding the fortune-telling rods. The old man rushed in, prostrated himself before the god, then got under the incense table. The people in the temple saw the bloody saber in his hand and took him for a murderer or some crazed husband who had just killed his wife. Frightened, they ran for help.

Presently, the officials in charge of the execution rushed into the temple. From them, the people learned that the old man was, in reality, in charge of watching the City Gate, and that he had just executed two people. The worshippers decided that for this reason he had gone mad. . . .[29]

If the worker in *Construction* is a Countryman dislocated in place, the executioner in *The New and the Old* is a Countryman dislocated in time. The play-acting involved in finding the executioner guilty and punishing him according to the strictures of earlier times, coupled with the fuss the citizens make when they discover the executioner hiding under the table, suggest the psychological and moral changes that have taken place with the passage of time. Traditionally, even lawful execution was normally held as unjust, and the executioner was held accountable to his victim. In one sense, this was fair play: execution of the criminal by law; punishment for the criminal's killer and a bonus for having enforced the law. In modern times, no killing is considered unjust. Furthermore, it is for show. Even the pretense of guilt is considered insane. Traditionally, the magistrate was revealed as a sadist who tried to rid himself of his own complicity by placing the stigma of responsibility on the executioner, and forthwith punishing him. In modern times, the official responsible for the execution luxuriates in the act by turning it into a spectacle. Han Shih-heng, a leftist critic during the Thirties, wrote in his article, "Mr. Shen Ts'ungwen's Fiction": "His fiction, generally speaking, deals with the trivial, insignificant things which happen to be interesting only to himself. Undoubtedly, his aim is to communicate this interest to his reader. Yet, no matter how delicately he deals with his subject matter, he doesn't inspire anything about the changes that have taken place in our society, and the sense of social responsibility we have...."[30] It is apparent that Han Shih-heng read Shen Ts'ung-wen only on the surface and didn't explore deeper than that surface, or, perhaps, he just didn't understand the multiple meanings submerged in the author's work. Shen Ts'ung-wen *is* concerned with the social conditions of his time. He eschews the ideological for the human point of view, as we can clearly see in *The New and the Old*. Or, as Shen himself wrote once in a letter to a poet, "A wise writer writes about the suffering of human beings with a smile."[31]

V *Eight Steeds*

For Shen Ts'ung-wen, the counterpart to the Countryman is the Cityman. *Eight Steeds* is about intellectuals in the city. The title refers to eight professors, but in an ironical sense. Mr. Ta-shih, one of the professors, teaches summer school at Tsingtao on the coast. There, the faculty members share lodgings in a

house which Mr. Ta-shih calls "Natural Clinic." He writes to
his fiancée: "I diagnose that they are sick—I am not joking.
Two of them are crazy.... They are learned scholars, but have
never enjoyed life. Even their desires are restrained and suppressed.... I will write to you about these respectable friends
of mine, one by one."[32] Mr. Ta-shih thinks himself qualified to
be a doctor, a spiritually and physically healthy man. The story
he tells is composed of the sketches of the eight intellectuals.
Professor A:

> On the small table in the room, there was a picture of the whole
> family: the man and the wife and six children. The wife was fat.
> On the bed hung with a white linen mosquito-net was a white
> pillow, embroidered with blue flowers. By the pillow, there were
> an old-fashioned flowered stomach warmer, a book called *Suspicion
> of the Rain*, another titled *Five Hundred Romantic Poems*. On the
> mosquito-net hung a cigarette poster of a half-naked beauty.
> On the window sill were a bottle of pills for the kidneys, a bottle
> of fish-liver pills, and an adhesive pad for headaches.[33]

The passage superbly sketches the surroundings and furnish-
ings of a petit-bourgeois middle-aged intellectual. According
to the author's customary taste and economy, we are quickly
given clues to the identity of Professor A: The formal family
picture with the fat wife and six children contrasts with the
cigarette poster of the half-naked beauty, which suggests an
ironic difference between the real life of Professor A and his
desires. The white pillow embroidered with flowers that contrasts with *Five Hundred Romantic Poems* suggests an ironic
and ambiguous blend of subtleties and vulgarities that comprise Professor A's character. These differences are a product
of his unnatural way of life, which causes him to have kidney
problems and headaches.

The author goes on to give sketches of the next five professors: B, C, D, E, and F from his conversations with them,
about which he faithfully reports to his fiancée.

Professor B has a wife and three children, all of whom he
abandoned by leaving his native home. He has never returned.
Because it is more convenient to his way of life, he prefers
living alone. When he is talking with Mr. Ta-shih on the beach,
he sees several girls in bathing suits.

The one wearing a red bathing suit had a shapely, plump figure and was very attractive. Her bare feet left beautiful prints on the wet sand. Professor B bent to pick up from one of the footprints a small oyster shell, lustrous like pearl, and wiped the sand from it with his fingers, gently and lecherously.[34]

Shen provides his reader with an understanding of Professor B's character without being heavy-handed—he provides him with the subtle and suppressed sensuality of this frustrated man in middle age. He is like a marionette in the author's deft hands, but a marionette sensitive to everything that goes on around him. He responds to *red* bathing suits, *bare* feet, *wet* sand, all of which activate the reader's senses, just as, in the story, they activated the character's.

Professor C speaks of platonic love between a man and a woman. The woman about whom he speaks was sick and went to see a doctor who suggested that her sickness stemmed from her unnatural relationship with her lover, and he suggested that she "set free the animality in her nature." She died. Her lover married. Asked for his opinions about love, Professor C answers that he is too old to have any opinion on the subject; but, at the same time, his eyes are fixed on a picture of Venus. He turns away only to inquire about an attractive girl in Mr. Ta-shih's class, a girl who also happens to be Professor C's niece. Then, he returns his eyes to the picture of Venus.

Dialogue is the main thing here. Most of it is devoted to the story of the platonic lovers. When the author turns to Freudian psychologizing vis-à-vis Professor C and his niece, not enough ground is covered, and Professor C emerges half-clothed, so to speak.

Each of the other three professors is, in his own way, sick in his attitude toward women. The seventh, Professor G, is the only healthy man in the "Natural Clinic." Mr. Ta-shih discovers why: he receives frequent visits from an attractive girl. Mr. Ta-shih describes the six sick professors in his letters to his fiancée, but keeps his impressions of Professor G and his girl friend, one whom Mr. Ta-shih finds attractive himself, in his notebook. He refrains from going to the girl in order to keep her and her lover from becoming "sick," or so he thinks. He intends to return to his fiancée the next day, the day that summer school ends. Then, as he is strolling along the beach, he finds some words written in the sand: "In this world, some don't know the ocean and don't love it; some do know it, but don't dare love it."[35] Farther on, he comes upon a pair of beautiful eyes etched in the wet sand. He decides to stay at the beach another three days.

While Mr. Ta-shih is waxing satirical about the other men's various sicknesses, we, as readers, learn the nature of the real neurosis. The author lets the reader scrutinize Mr. Ta-shih while Mr. Ta-shih himself is scrutinizing the others. The story, thus, has a double irony, made lucid by a double point of view. How far can we trust the central intelligence? Can we trust it at all? But, for all that, the author never condescends, never lets on that our "doctor," Mr. Ta-shih, is to be despised for his obsession. We may take the story in light of what Shen gives us: dialogue, gesture, and objects; or we may glean another theme from what Mr. Ta-shih's fiancée writes in a letter to him: "I have read your sketch of Professor F. You must have made it larger than life. You wrote about what he had said. It doesn't sound to me like what he would say. But I believe that you were trying to be honest in your portrait of him,... This sketch, like the others, has its own style, which makes the character real on paper...."[36]

Shen Ts'ung-wen is not at his best when he deals with the Cityman. He is more powerful with his Countryman. His Citymen are stereotypes, because he has, always, it seems, the notion of Countryman in mind, a standard against which he measures other character types.

VI *The Border Town*

The Border Town, a novelette, is representative of Shen Ts'ung-wen's notions of what constitutes an ideal world, unspoiled by modern civilization, for his Countryman. Here, the author's intention is to present his reader with an impressionistic backdrop to his story: the landscape, the town, the customs, the people—all are harmoniously rendered in light and shadow.

The river was once known as the Yu River, famous in history; but now it was called the White River. At Ch'en-chou, this river met the Yüan River, and joined its own purity to the muddy waters of the greater river. If you went upstream, you would find drop-offs where the water was so pure you could see the bottom forty or fifty feet below the surface, and when the sun was shining you could even see the white pebbles and the small red stones, and watch the fishes gliding in the water as if floating in the air. Along the banks there were great mountains shrouded in slender bamboo, used for making paper. The bamboo remained a deep vivid green all the year round. The houses near the river were surrounded by peach and apricot groves, so that in spring wherever there were peach blossoms, there were also houses, and wherever there were houses, there was wine. In summer, you could distinguish the houses by the purple flowered clothes which were hung out to dry in the sun. When autumn and winter came, the houses stood out against the cliffs and along the riverside. You would see them shining clear in the distance with their yellow mud walls and black roof tiles, all perfectly placed in harmony with their surroundings. . . .[37]

In such a world, "even the prostitutes were genuine people," and "the people knew of the existence of soldiers only because they could hear a bugler who went to blow his bugle for fun on the city wall."[37] Shen Ts'ung-wen, the sculptor in *Three Men and a Girl*, becomes a painter in *The Border Town*. His characters here are just sketches. It seems that he does not want to dig deeper into them: he loves them too much.

The old ferryman was arguing with the paper-seller on the ferry. He refused to take the fare which the paper-seller offered him. He seemed offended. He forced the paper-seller to take the money back. When the ferryman had directed the ferry to the opposite bank, the paper-seller jumped to the dock, threw the coins to the ferryman and hurried away, smiling. The old ferryman was keeping the ferry steady to let another passenger off and couldn't give chase. He called his granddaughter who was on the hill.
"Ts'ui-ts'ui, Ts'ui-ts'ui! Get that man! Don't let him go!"
The girl didn't know what had happened, and she ran with her yellow dog to stop the man. The man laughed, "Please don't stop me. . . ."
The next passenger came and told Ts'ui-ts'ui what had happened. She still held the first man by the arm, however, crying, "No! No! I can't let you go." The yellow dog was barking as if in agreement. Now the passengers were laughing. The grandfather ran up, breath-

ing hard. He squeezed the coins into the man's hand, and put a big
bunch of tobacco in his basket. He said, smiling and rubbing his
hands together, "Go now. All of you." All of them left, laughing.
"Grandpa, I thought that man had stolen something, or was
fighting with you," Ts'ui-ts'ui said.
"No," said the grandfather. "He gave me too much money. I told
him I didn't want it. But he argued with me. He's not a reasonable
man."
'You gave him back all the money?"
The grandfather shook his head, his lips pressed together, one
eye closed, trying to smile slyly, victoriously; he took the string of
coins which hung from his trouser's belt and gave it to Ts'ui-ts'ui.
"The tobacco he got from us will be enough for him to smoke until
he gets to town."[39]

The Border Town is fraught with such delightful sketches.
Its people are honest and simple, although tragic. They are
run-of-the-mill, simple characters, and like children, they still
have a lot of growing up to do. Their existence is frozen. The
story is therefore very light, very agreeable, as a sort of antidote
for the ills of one inured to a more modern life. As art, it is
not among Shen Ts'ung-wen's best work. The author likes the
story, perhaps because of his nostalgia for the lost land. He
defends the story in his article *Exercise.*

The Border Town is like a small house, which takes little material,
occupies little space, economizes on everything, but does not lack
air and sunlight. What I want to express is a form of life which
is fine, healthy, natural, and not against human nature. My intention is not to take the reader on a tour round T'ao-yüan. I want to
take a few ordinary people who live in the small town in the Yu
River area in order to show the reader how they live their share of
sorrow and happiness when involved in a human affair, thus giving
an accurate interpretation of the word love. . . .[40]

VII *Mire*

When Shen Ts'ung-wen talks about the unusual love he
has for the Countrymen in his preface to *The Border Town,* he
says:

I also want to give the reader a different kind of story for contrast: a story about Countrymen who are distorted by wars and

revolutions, who have lost their simple, diligent and peaceful qualities. . . . I want to write simply and honestly about those small people's instinct to survive and their means of survival when the country is propelled by history toward an unknown fate. . . .[41]

Mire, then, is a story about these "small people." They are, however, unlike the "transplants" Shen Ts'ung-wen writes about in the previous stories we have discussed. In *Mire*, a group of poor deprived people live in the slums close to a factory and a jail. Smallpox is prevalent. Many people have died of the disease. At the same time, the area is flooded by the unchecked ditches flowing from the factory's waste disposal unit. The community representatives demand that the factory management do something about the flood problem, but management refuses. Soon after, a fire breaks out in the slums. Many of the community's residents are left homeless. The flood abates only when water from the factory is used to fight the fire.

Mire's real hero is its crowd of people. For a time, the character of a woman seems central to the story. We follow her from the beginning through to the end, along an obstacle course that seems especially constructed to trip her up: the smallpox, the flood, and the fire. We first see her at a pawn-shop, trying to obtain money for medicine for her son who is dying from the pox; our last glimpse of her is at the coffin of a man, Secretary Chang, who died in the fire. Her seemingly central role notwithstanding, the woman's character is never fully developed. Secretary Chang, who is almost always seen through the eyes of other characters, and who never addresses himself directly to the reader, except when the people go to the factory to complain about the flood, is nevertheless a more fully realized character. He has been a farmer, an army sergeant (a position he lost after the revolution), and in the slums has become a kind of intellectual leader who helps educate the illiterate. He is an opium addict, but is too poor to feed his habit, except with opium ashes he gets from the patrol police chief who smokes with him occasionally. Secretary Chang is always eager to help others. He is killed in the fire after he has been "running around like a crazy dog" to help children, chickens and cats escape the flames. Shen doesn't focus on the Secretary's character, however, until after his death.

The man who was an official of the charity organization opened the door of his office and asked the people who were waiting to take the coffin for the name of the deceased. One of them answered, "Secretary Chang."
The official of the charity organization, whose name was also Chang, asked impatiently, "What? Who's called Secretary Chang?"
"Every one called him Secretary Chang."
The official Chang was angry. "The coffins here are not for your Secretary Chang. We don't have a single board to make a coffin. Go talk to the District Chief. We are not making coffins for any Secretary. This charity organization is for the poor." Then he added, "Ask him to come himself. I want to see that Secretary."
The merchant, who had come in with the living Chang, understood that he didn't like the coincidence of names, and he said, "Sir, they don't understand what you said. He was called Secretary Chang because he used to write letters for people. You may register him as anyone you like. He was a flexible man in life; he must be an amiable ghost, now that he is dead. He wouldn't care which name was given the coffin registry."[42]

The above passage offers us a duality: the man who fears death, and the man who is not recognized as an individual even after he is dead. In fact, the author gives the reader very little opportunity to know Secretary Chang until after he is dead. He goes on to write of the dead man:

The so-called coffin was but a long box made of rough unfinished boards. It was too short for the hero, so they had to bend his legs a little before they could put him into it. The people standing around were silent. Tsu-kuei, who was nailing the corners of the coffin with a hammer, saw a fragment of the faded uniform of the former sergeant through an opening in the coffin lid. . . .[43]

The bent legs in the coffin and the fragment of worn-out uniform showing through the opening of the coffin are epiphanies: this man, whose fate was death, has no identity and has to be shaped for his grave, even when he is dead. Only the glimpse of his uniform showing through the coffin opening reminds people of who he was:

It was getting dark when the woman headed for home. She heard the gongs and thought that they came from the Taoist monks praying for the good man who had just been killed. She was thinking that anyway, this man died with such honor and to such a grandiose service. . . . As she walked farther along, she found out that the gongs did not come from the monks, but from some other, far away place. Standing behind her house, she watched the unpainted coffin silhouetted against the darkness by the edge of the flood waters, shimmering cold. No one was there.[44]

Even the grandiose service for Secretary Chang turns out to be an illusion. Secretary Chang represents the old society with all its good and bad which has now been lost forever because of the spread of an industrial civilization. Whenever the author deals with this character, he is superb. But he does not focus his story on the character of Secretary Chang. He might have made him the main character of the story, and followed him through participation in the chaotic events of smallpox, flood and fire, from beginning to end, and Secretary Chang as a character might then have been an equivalent of Lu Hsün's Ah Q.

CHAPTER 9

A Critique (II): Themes, Imagery, and Style in Shen Ts'ung-wen's Fiction

IN *Apocalypse,* a later novel, D. H. Lawrence wrote: "what we want is to ... re-establish the living organic connections, with the cosmos, the sun and earth, with mankind and nation and family. Start with the sun, and the rest will slowly, slowly happen...."[1] Like Lawrence, Shen Ts'ung-wen contends that to live is to obey the rhythms involving all nature. Disharmony occurs, Shen Ts'ung-wen believes, when man fails to keep within that complex of natural rhythms. However exacting it may be, nature in Lawrence's and Shen's world is not the gloomy parent that inhabits Thomas Hardy's works: a frowning, capricious nature that periodically molests human beings. For Shen Ts'ung-wen, nature personifies abundance, vitality—the spontaneous life force; something totally indifferent to reason, civilization, and history. It is this spontaneous life force that has enabled the Chinese people to survive several thousand years of war, revolution and natural disaster. On the other hand, nature, when suppressed, can become quite destructive. This other view of nature may explain the duality in the Chinese character: the peaceful and the violent. Like many Chinese painted scrolls, the Chinese people are pacific—like clear mountain streams, calm waters. Beneath that placidity and resignation, however, there also lies the violence of thunderstorms. Many of Shen Ts'ung-wen's stories deal with the spontaneous life force of the natural people, while others treat of men and women, who in a very literal sense, are not acclimated: men and women who have been ill-used by modern civilization. For them, nature is inimical. Shen Ts'ung-wen's favorite themes concern nature in its various moods of abundance, violence, and innocence.

Shen Ts'ung-wen is not only a humanist; he is also a stylist. One of his contemporaries, Su Hsueh-lin, has said, "His language, though sometimes awkward, never depends on clichés; it is always free, lively, very expressive of his nature . . . . From quite ordinary material, he can produce extraordinary results. . . . His sentences are compressed, sharp. . . . Everything he does has the beauty of simplicity. . . . "[2] Laudatory as Su's remarks may be, they reveal only the bare surface of Shen Ts'ung-wen's accomplishments as prose stylist. Indeed, critics have yet to appraise Shen as a *modern* writer. Scant attention has been paid to his craftsmanship in imagery and symbolism, which give his language a density and the texture, frequently, of poetry. Instead, much has been made of Shen Ts'ung-wen's "simplicity" and "straightforward narrative." Calling Shen's style simple, without further elaboration, is not enough. Critics often equate a difficult style with complexity of meaning, ignoring the fact that a simple style may not only possess its depth of meaning, but more importantly, conceal its own symmetry. Perhaps as a tribute to Shen Ts'ung-wen's "simplicity," critics have chosen to read him on one level only; and on this level, everything is plain, formal, and direct. But another level remains—internal, elusive, but with an irresistible tug. It is on this second level that one discovers the complexity of meaning. Shen Ts'ung-wen's sentences may appear awkward at times, and deceptively random, but they have a tonal effect, with themes submerged in imagery. "Language," Shen once wrote, "can only achieve color and brilliance *after* organization." He also maintained that his writing was the "physical exercise of emotions," and that "a writer who is used to physical exercise of emotions must feel that it is easier to serve words than women."[3] Shen's language is spontaneous: it is expansive, unvarnished, sensuous, and appeals to all the senses at once. It is this language—the language of poetry—that he uses with increasing facility in almost every literary form.

Shen Ts'ung-wen's remarks in the preface to a collection of short stories, *Ah-chin,* explain very well his attitude toward writing:

You may appreciate the freshness of my stories, but usually overlook the passion hidden in them; you may appreciate the simplicity

of my language, but usually overlook the sorrow and pain hidden
in the works. . . . You want the work to have "thought," "blood,"
and "tears"; you want the work to specifically express all these
elements in the development of the story, in the speech of the
characters, even on the cover of the book. What you ask for is easy
to give. But I cannot give you what you ask for. My writing does
not have this or that. I don't understand all the kind of "thought"
you talk about. . . . When we come to this point, I feel very much
alone. . . ."4

I *The Lovers*
(*A Bunch of Wild Flowers*)

Huang, the cityman, goes to live in a village to nurse his
delicate constitution. He hears people shouting that they have
caught a couple of "things." He is shocked to find, instead of
the two live boars he expected to be the catch, a man and a
woman. Some villagers are also on hand to witness the scene.
The woman captured is wearing a bunch of wild flowers round
her head as a sign of sin. Huang is told that someone walking
near the mountain came upon the young couple in the valley
and they were in a most compromising position. The couple
have been caught and are now exhibited in the public square.
A tipsy man teases and insults the captives. A man who has
the manner and bearing of an officer begins to interrogate the
woman. His tone is flamboyant. She does not reply. The crowd
is agitated. With fiendish relish, the crowd demands, "Whip
them, weight them down with stones and cast them into the
pond, or refresh the man with urine and feed the woman cow
dung." The officer, who is a local judge, now discovers that the
much maligned couple are actually newlyweds. They were on
their way home to visit the woman's parents when the temperate
weather, a most tempting haystack, and the flowers on the mountain trail stopped them. They proceeded to do what young lovers
normally do. It was then that they were caught by the villagers.
The officer and the drunken man refuse to release the prisoners.
Finally, after Huang's intercession, the local base commander,
realizing what has happened, steps in and releases them. When
the couple leave, Huang asks the woman for the wild flowers
as a memento of the incident.

Nature blasphemed and redeemed is the underlying theme

of the story. As he has shown in other stories, Shen Ts'ung-wen wastes no time in elaborate introduction-building, but immediately projects his image of the wild flowers. "He was even more shocked when he stepped closer and found that a couple were bound. They were country people, very young. The woman was silently weeping before the merciless scrutiny of the crowd. She was wearing a bunch of wild flowers round her head. The flowers fluttered in the breeze whenever she moved her head. Under different circumstances, the crown would have been graceful."[5]

The first time Paul and Clara make love in D. H. Lawrence's *Sons and Lovers,* petals of carnations are strewn over Clara's body and over the ground where the two make love. The wild flowers that crown Shen Ts'ung-wen's young bride in *The Lovers* and the red carnations on Clara reflect the same life force. That image is heightened and reintroduced throughout the story. It is also extended and developed through the allusion to live boars, which are properties of nature. Shen Ts'ung-wen's life force is mostly represented by nature and animals. Just as the young couple is addressed by members of the crowd as "things" (an address intended to debase them), they are also children of nature, since the flowers that adorn them externalize some kind of wild sweetness in their innate beings.

Instant characterization is achieved in the author's choice of idiom for the villagers and the cityman. When they talk about the youthful captives, the characters' instinctive associations are "live boars" and "things." Swiftly, economically, the author presents his reader with the villagers' and the cityman's contemptuous attitude toward nature.

They caught them all right. But now what would they do with them? The captors didn't want to be responsible.

Since the couple had been caught, they would have to confront the county chief who would sit in front of the table covered with a red table cloth, wearing dark glasses, and try them. But why had they been caught? Captors and captives alike were in the dark....[6]

The villagers represent a tribal code, a mindless reflex moored in ancient Confucianism. They are incapable of understanding what it is they wish to punish.

The man captured lowered his head and saw Huang's black shoes. They were not objects he was accustomed to. Although he could not shake off his present predicament, he was practically hypnotized by those square-toed, black leather shoes. When Huang asked him where he was from, he sensed that Huang was sympathetic, and lifted his eyes to look at him. He shook his head and smiled, meaning that he was being unfairly treated.[7]

The square-toed, black leather shoes, alien to the Countryman, symbolize civilization and also serve as "black" warning. Once more, the Countryman is a stranger for whom no explanation is made. Once again, his whole history is stated by his smile. "Huang looked at the woman again. Not twenty yet, she was in a clean, moon-blue linen dress, bleached and hanging crisply from her body. Her face wore a habitual flush. She was slender, graceful, as if she did not come from the country at all. . . ."[8]

As this passage indicates, Shen Ts'ung-wen is a very sensuous writer. He woos the reader into a rather otherworldly atmosphere, then activates his senses with an almost palpable barrage: the blue cloth material denotes the blueness of the moon; the bleach smell carries the imprint of the sun; the crudeness of the linen dress furnishes the rough touch of the countryside. Each physical detail contains its reference to nature.

From the throng surrounding the couple, a man with a spotty face and a thick red nose advanced. He looked drunk, as if he had just left his drink and came to watch the scene. With his big, hairy hand, he touched the woman's cheek. He talked to himself, saying that the captives should be stripped, whipped with bramble vines and dragged before the county chief. . . . This drunken man was diverted, fortunately, by someone in the crowd who pulled at his trousers and said that a cityman was present. . . .[9]

In Shen Ts'ung-wen's account of the nimble interplay of human behavior, natural life force, represented by the floral crown, is tainted with sensuality, represented by the drunken man with the spotty face and the thick red nose (nature's perversion). His crude manner, hairy hands, trouser hitching, all suggest sensuality which is relieved only by the incongruous presence of the cityman.

This ill-mixed group is soon joined by the guard leader whose "gestures ape those of barracks officers at military parades in the city." He plucks a grass switch and flicks it across the young man's face. He interrogates the couple in the tone of a customs officer.

> The woman did not answer. She lifted her head, first to the questioner's face, then to Huang's. Meekly, she looked down again at her feet, which wore phoenix embroidered shoes. In the same flamboyant tone, the officer asked, "Where are you from? If you don't tell me, I'll have someone drag you down to the district court!"[10]

Through the guard leader we feel the law's impudence and its abuse. As the law's representative, the guard leader flicks his grass switch across the young man's face—the face of the "criminal." But frivolous interrogatory manners define him for what he really is, a man no better than the rednosed drunk. The young woman's embroidered shoes hint of desire, a desire to flout convention, and pertain to the villagers, whose rigidity is concealed within an attraction to the very objects which spell violation of the moral code.

As so often happens in Shen Ts'ung-wen's more finely quilted stories, innocent little overtures can and do transcend their surface inanities. Huang and the guard leader are limbs of one rotting tree, namely city government, and law—and yet the two men are as different from each other as night is from day. Huang represents authority under probation; in the guard leader is invested law's irascibility and impunity. Huang comes from the city, but cannot fully imbibe its rawness; the guard leader drools over his memories of city parades and is loath to leave the company of barracks officers who conduct them. His irresolution—his irresolute character—notwithstanding, Huang gives head to the concept of law. Each man is in his own way essential to the administrative machinery governing the law—the guard as implementor and Huang as conscience.

> The guard leader, apparently because he appreciated what Huang had done, said to the young woman, "You should thank the gentleman. It was kind of him to speak for you."
> The woman was removing the bunch of wild flowers which the villagers had wound about her head as a sign of sin. She bowed to

Huang. In her hands was the bunch of wild flowers. She didn't throw them away. . . .[11]

With candor and delicacy, the author focuses once more on the wild flowers. The young bride has been manhandled, slandered and threatened with all manner of indignity. But she does not protest: she is inviolate. She clutches her bouquet, as she will always cling to anything that belongs to nature.

Standing alone by a small bridge at the foot of the hill, Huang inhaled the fragrance of the flowers wafted by the wind. Something in him dictated that he must retain a memento of what had happened. Thinking of the wild flowers in the woman's hand, he called after her. "Slow down, please. And drop your flowers on the ground—for me."[12]

The life force, that unknown and elusive quality, symbolized by the wild flowers, is what Huang, the urban castoff, craves and what he needs for rejuvenation. This is Shen Ts'ung-wen's coronation in nature. The moment is infinitely moving, like the ritual passing of the torch from hand to hand. In the transference, a nymph of nature has confirmed its scent and inviolability, while conferring salvation on another. If civilization, with its preponderance of customs and traditions, is myopic in its justice, it is not altogether blind: there will always be a Huang to grope for more humane guidelines. Meanwhile, the Countryman will prevail, at least in Shen Ts'ung-wen's work; his angelic smile will abide forever.

II *Po-tzu*
(*Hairy Legs That Sing*)

In *Random Sketches on a Trip to West Hunan*, Shen Ts'ung-wen writes of the lives of river boatmen:

The strange thing is that these boatmen have become marvelously adept at skirting torrents and whirls. They live on the water, and understand more than ordinary people do the terrors of water. In order to survive, they are prepared to jump into the water at every moment of the day. When the small boat goes up the torrents, they have to plunge into the white waves. Yet they always find a way out of them. . . .[13]

Po-tzu is about such a boatman, a man who hurries ashore to keep a rendezvous with a prostitute. The story is divided into four sections: the first depicts the river and the shore of Ch'en-chou, and the boatmen who sing as they work high in the rigging of the ships; the second follows Po-tzu to his tryst with the prostitute; the third concerns Po-tzu's reboarding of his ship; the fourth concerns the ship's departure.

The opening paragraph of the story shows Shen at his descriptive best:

On every bow and stern of every ship, there were people standing about; they were clad in blue sweaters; they puffed at long bamboo pipes; their hands and feet were exposed to the wind—hands and feet so hairy they resembled the hairy hands and feet of those cave elves in children's fantasies. Seeing such hands and feet, one remembered the names of heroes, such as "Flying Hairy Legs." These people were like movable pulleys working up and down the masts. When it was not possible to pull or drag the ropes, you would see the wonder of these hairy legs. Up the smooth, bare masts, they seemed almost to fly. To show us perhaps that this was only child's play, these young boatmen sang of their labors as they unlooped cords. If there were other boatmen on other masts, they would sing songs in response to each other. . . .[14]

Lively, and somewhat playful, Shen's opening also incorporates other technical devices to establish both tone and theme. The key phrase is "hairy legs," which describes the legs of the boatmen: hairy and fluffy hands and feet, hairy hands and feet of the elves in magic caves, hairy legs that fly. The list virtually trembles with animal appendages: hair and the implied ability to fly; and these qualities are amplified by the desire that sings.

The singing stopped. When a red wind lamp was lit, the singer was at the audience's side. . . .
Like the other boatmen, Po-tzu carefully walked on the gangplank and went ashore, with his cloth trouser's belt used as a wallet full of coins. He was walking along the muddy beach. There was no moon, there was no stars. It was drizzling rain. His feet slowly stirred in the mud, until they became heavy with it, and he could barely move. He walked toward the red light in the small, multi-storied house on a street near the riverside. . . .

When the door swung open, a muddy leg was thrust inside, and the body of the woman was embraced by two strong arms. His newly shaven face which had been exposed to the rain and sun was nuzzled by a broad, warm face.[15]

The author uses cinematic closeups of muddy legs, a device which recurs until the legs are transformed into live little animals which impose upon the story a naturalistic atmosphere checked only by what is essentially the formal structure of the story. Frame after frame (since we are using cinematic terms) is accomplished in the language of the symbol. Po-tzu's progress to the prostitute's room from the riverside is shown mainly through the hero's muddy legs: slowly moving legs become muddy feet, one of which seems impeded outside the door, while the other advances across the threshold. Two different images inhabit the same pair of muddy legs in what may be construed to be a Jekyll-and-Hyde denouement; the former suggests lust—the latter hints at Po-tzu's indecisive joy, simultaneously creating an impression of strength and violence. "Po-tzu was standing under the red lamp which colored the whole room with its light. The woman was looking at him, smiling. They were facing each other. Po-tzu was the taller. He crouched and took her by the waist as though pulling oars; she leaned toward him."[16]

From the red wind lamp which illuminates rain and river, to the red lamp which illuminates the room, the color scheme reflects two different feelings, two different scenes, two different atmospheres. The story advances with the shift from wind lamp to brothel lamp. Po-tzu took the woman, and they fell into the bed. "The lamp is bright, illuminating a bunch of muddy footprints on the yellow floor."[17] The sentence is a complete paragraph in itself, and the first section of the story ends with it. Its simplicity is deceptive, for it covers a lot of territory. The cinematic closeups of muddy legs are an integral part of the first section of the story. At section's close, when the lamp is bright (the author still uses the lamp as a device for the shifts from frame to frame), a bunch of muddy footprints replace the muddy legs in the closeup. These muddy footprints conjure an image of animals: nocturnal, with the energy and desire of wolf and tiger.

A contemporary of Shen Ts'ung-wen, critic Han Shih-heng (*Selected Essays of Literary Criticism*) compares the author to

Chang Tzu-p'ing, a writer of popular pulp and pornography. Han Shih-heng contends that the main difference between the two lies in their treatment of sexual relationships; Shen Ts'ung-wen's being mnemonic and suggestive as opposed to Chang's somewhat more explosive descriptions. Han Shih-heng goes on to say that Shen Ts'ung-wen is a more effective writer in exciting a reader's instincts. He thinks that this only makes Shen Ts'ung-wen more "dangerous." While this may be considered damning with faint praise, the critic does acknowledge Shen Ts'ung-wen's technical abilities, and his accomplishment in achieving a desired effect via mnemonic and suggestive techniques.

The second section of the story refers initially to Po-tzu's footprints: "Po-tzu's crisscrossed footprints dried and were more sharply etched on the floor than before. The light shone, as usual, on the two bodies lying on the bed."[18]

From soggy footprints to dried footprints, the two closeups, accomplished with both taste and economy, prepare us for the scene in bed—the evolution of time and character. The second section of the story largely concerns Po-tzu and flirtation with the prostitute.

"Po-tzu, I say you are a bull."
"If I ain't you won't believe I behaved myself down the river."
"You behaved yourself! Do you dare swear you're clean enough to enter the Temple of Heaven?"
"Well, maybe your mother believes in oaths. I don't."[19]

This is the carefree, gritty language of the people who live on the waters. It is the kind of language Shen Ts'ung-wen knows very well, the kind he mentions in an essay, *My Writing and the Waters*: "If there is anything noticeable in my style, it is because I remember a lot about the language of the people who live on the waters."[20] In the dialogue quoted above, even the endearments are animalistic (bull). Like the muddy footprints, the endearment "bull" suggests the animal energy and desire of Po-tzu. The second section of the story ends with a closeup of the muddy legs again: "By the bedside dangled Po-tzu's muddy legs, and wound around the upper part of his legs were tiny feet in red silk slippers."[21] The dangling legs suggest the slackening of desire; the tiny feet in red silk slippers signify desire's continuation.

In the story's third section, Po-tzu returns aboard ship, holding a torch. With him, too, lingers the memory of flesh—"The woman's movements and her laughter are like leeches nailed to his heart." Shen Ts'ung-wen's prose manner repeatedly conveys desire through animalistic imagery. The *leeches nailed* in the heart: Leeches of course suggest an almost unshakable obstinacy, and sliminess; *nailed* heightens the effect in its myriad connotations—sharpness, deep penetration, and so forth. Desire is like a leech; it will not easily let go; and desire can deeply penetrate a man's flesh: "Softly singing 'The Great Wall' and 'Playing Jade Cards,' he gingerly walked over the gangplank to the ship, but suddenly stopped singing 'Eighteen Caresses,' because he heard a woman's voice coaxing a baby, and he heard the sound of a mouth suckling milk. The wife of the ship master was feeding her own little boss."[22]

In bed, Po-tzu bit the whore's breast. Now, he comes upon a child suckling. Mother and prostitute are kinfolk. The mother's breast is a life source. So is the prostitute's breast: each gives life. Of the river people, Shen Ts'ung-wen has said: "I feel that their desire and sorrow are both very saintly." Mud, milk, the river, the rain: life is a cycle, and everything must eventually flow back to its original source.

Logically, the story should end with the image of the child suckling the mother's breast. Inexplicably, the author writes an additional section with Po-tzu going ashore twice more before the departure of the junk. One feels that after that thematic coda containing the mother-and-child scene, anything else in the story is gratuitous. Since the preceding sections are already integral parts and fuse into a compact whole, the reader wonders why the author saw fit to append material which could only be extraneous, and therefore create an imbalance in the structure of the story.

Given its textural density, its psychological interplay, its almost breathless flair for the symbol, *Po-Tzu* still does not measure up to a story like *Three Men and a Girl*, whose built-in symbolism and inviolable theme transcend its more self-conscious meanings. Happily, in almost everything Shen Ts'ung-wen

touches, his all-embracing humanity shines through and trans-
forms even the least promising material so that it assumes a
dimension of its own.

III *Quiet*
(*The Peach Blossoms in the Small Buddhist Convent*)

Quiet details the experiences of a family of war refugees
stranded in a small town. The mother of the family is seriously
ill in bed; her eldest daughter and her daughter-in-law are out
to consult a fortune teller about the plight of the family. The
maid is doing laundry in the courtyard. The fourteen-year-old
girl, Yüeh-min, and her nephew, the small boy, Pei-sheng, are
left alone; they enjoy sitting on the shabby terrace, watching
the natural world: the sprouts of grapevines growing out of
crevices between the stones, the clear river, the kites in the blue
sky, the green riverside with flowers, the vegetable gardens, the
peach blossoms beyond the red walls of the small Buddhist convent, the grazing horses and the men who tend them. They are
happy on the terrace. Downstairs, however, they must confront
reality: threats of war and death. When they return to the terrace, the natural world is out of reach. They come and go, and
the drama of the story fluctuates between a quiet natural life
force and threats of war and death. Following are some passages
from the story about the natural world seen from the terrace.

In a while, a small nun came out of the small Buddhist convent
where there were peach blossoms. She wore a black cap and a gray
gown; she was carrying a new bamboo basket. She walked across
the grassland toward the river. Reaching a spot close to the ferry
slip, she stopped, climbed onto a stone, and crouching there, slowly
rolled up her sleeves. She looked around a while, then glanced at
the kites in the sky before casually taking out a big bunch of
vegetables from her basket. The river stirred with a beautiful shimmering. . . .
After washing the vegetables, the nun began to wash a piece of
cloth, or a dress, by beating it with a wooden rod. This accomplished,
she shook the cloth out in the water and began to beat it again. The
sound of the beating was echoed by the city wall. The nun must
have been amused by the echo, because she stopped washing and
yelled in a shrill voice: "Szu-lin! Szu-lin!" The wall responded,

"Szu-lin! Szu-lin!" Then, a shrill voice called from the convent, "Szu-lin! Szu-lin!" That voice said something else, perhaps asked whether the nun had finished her washing. It developed that Szu-lin was the nun's name. Since she had done her washing and had had fun by the river, she picked up the basket and turned to go. She seemed to intentionally walk across the white cloth which she had spread on the grass to dry.[23]

Here again, Shen Ts'ung-wen is direct, very sensuous and visual in his approach to scene. The simplicity of his language itself is symbolic of the quietness of the natural life force. Shen Ts'ung-wen's natural world—the peach blossoms, the river, the vegetables, the echo of the nun's name—each stands in its unique identity and has absolute individuality, or "otherness." Individuality is the natural form of things and human beings. One creature will be in harmony with another only when it realizes its "otherness." The girl and the little boy go to the terrace because they like to be in a world where their own otherness, as well as nature's, exists harmoniously. Following is a passage from the "downstairs" world.

When she (Yüeh-min) went into the room, she saw her mother lying in bed, as quiet as a corpse, breathing weakly; her face, thin and small, showed fatigue and sorrow. It seemed that she had been awake a while. When she heard the footsteps in the room, she opened her eyes.

"Yüeh-min, would you look and see whether there is some water in the thermos bottle?"

Pouring hot water to mix with medicine for the patient, Yüeh-min watched her mother's face which was getting thinner every day. She said, "Mother, it's a lovely day. From the terrace, I saw the peach blossoms blooming in the small convent across the river."

The patient didn't say a word, but merely smiled. Remembering the blood she had coughed a moment before, she reached out with her thin hand to feel her own forehead, speaking to herself, "I have no fever." Then, she smiled at the girl tenderly. The smile was so pathetically faint that the girl sighed.

"Is your cough better, mother?"

"Yes, yes it is. It doesn't matter. I don't feel weak. It was my fault. This morning I ate fish. Now, I've got a sore throat. But it doesn't matter."

While talking to her mother, the girl wanted to go over to have a look at the small spittoon by the pillow. The patient read her thoughts, and said, "There is nothing." Then she added, "Yüeh-min, you stand there and don't move. Let me see. You've grown up a lot recently. You look like a woman!"

Bashfully, Yüeh-min smiled. "Mother, do I look like a bamboo? I am worried. I'm too tall for a fourteen-year-old girl. It's not right. If I'm too tall, people will laugh at me."[24]

Soon, they begin to talk about their dreams of the ship and the father who is in the army and is supposed to come to take them any moment. Gently, obliquely, mother and daughter reach out to each other, and we, as readers, discover the symbolic undertones of two different worlds: the natural world (represented by the girl; the peach blossoms in the small convent garden; the girl's resemblance to the bamboo shoot) and the world of death and war (represented by the mother; the blood she coughs; her dream of the ship that will take the family to a safe place).

At the story's end, the girl hears the door bell ringing and thinks it may be her father who has come at last. Then, it is quiet again.

The girl was smiling. The slanting sunlight cast the shadow of the corner of the roof and the pole of the terrace on the courtyard. The shadow was in the shape of the paper flag which was planted on the grave of her father whom she was expecting.[25]

These lines, subdued and elegiac, are typical of Shen Ts'ung-wen's prose: simple, direct, yet ominous. The passage itself seems a triumph of understatement. The girl's smile is the cue to (1) psychological understatement: the girl smiles at the world beyond reach, the world she's seen from the terrace; (2) ironic understatement: the contrast between what the girl's smile suggests and reality—the father's grave; (3) symbolic understatement: natural life force, represented by the girl's smile in a war-death ravaged world, represented by the paper flag on the father's grave.

Quiet proclaims Shen Ts'ung-wen's accomplishments as an imagist, as an ironic structuralist, and as a master of physically and psychologically rich character. It also proclaims the power of his poetic language, symbolic of the quietness in which the natural life force dwells.

IV Hsiao-Hsiao
(Spotty Dog and Caterpillar)

Hsiao-hsiao is a story about a country girl of twelve who is married to a boy of three. She is rapidly developing into a woman while her husband is still very young. Her duty is to take care of her young husband and to work on the farm. Each day, she takes him to the farm with her, plays with him, feeds him, listens to him sing an erotic folk song which Spotty Dog, a farmhand, taught him. Hsiao-hsiao, the young wife, does not quite understand. Spotty Dog begins to flirt with her in a way that she does not quite understand either. When she is older, however, she begins to understand what Spotty Dog means when he tries to approach her through her husband, by playing with him, and singing the songs which make her blush. One spring day, she gives herself to Spotty Dog. When Spotty Dog later discovers that Hsiao-hsiao is pregnant, he runs away. Hsiao-hsiao does not like the fact that something is growing in her belly. She tries to run away, too. But her secret is discovered by her husband's family. The family feels itself disgraced, and to punish Hsiao-hsiao decide to marry her to someone else, all the while trying to keep the young husband away from her. Since no one wants her, she must stay with the family. Gradually, disgrace seems forgotten by the family, and once again, the young husband is permitted to go to his wife. Hsiao-hsiao gives birth to a boy. When she begins to sleep with her husband, her son is ten years old. He, in turn, marries a girl of eighteen years, when he is only twelve.

Hsaio-hsaio deals with the innocence of nature in contrast to Shen's conception of Confucian society. The author uses a style that neatly parallels his theme: a straightforward narrative rich in natural image and metaphor. Hsiao-hsiao's lover, Spotty Dog, of course, represents animal desire. Hsiao-hsiao is described as a "plant with sturdy *branches* and *leaves* growing up unnoticed in a corner of the *garden*." And "her mother-in-law was a pair of scissors that *cut off* all of Hsiao-hsiao's chances to grow.

Nevertheless, the girl couldn't be stopped when the *sun* and the *air* in the country made her grow."[26]

The small husband was always happy to see Spotty Dog. He wanted Spotty Dog to make a bug with the grass blades or a flute and a whistle with the bamboo. Spotty Dog tried to send him away, tried to sit down beside Hsiao-hsiao so he could sing songs to make her blush. Sometimes she was frightened and tried to keep her small husband around; other times, it seemed better to have Spotty Dog around and send her small husband away. One day, Spotty Dog made Hsiao-hsiao a woman.

At that moment, the small husband went down the hill to pluck berries. Spotty Dog, after he had sung several songs to Hsiao-hsiao, said that he had often thought of her in the past two years, and that he couldn't go to sleep at night for thinking of her, and he swore that he would never let anyone know what was about to happen between them. Hsiao-hsiao still didn't understand what he meant. Spotty Dog began to sing again. Hsiao-hsiao wanted him to swear an oath. The swearing made her feel secure. Then she gave in. When the small husband returned to her, she found *his hand swollen from the bite of a caterpillar. She held the small hand, blew at it and sucked it,* and when she thought about what had just happened, she realized that something was wrong.[27] (italics mine)

These passages are among Shen Ts'ung-wen's best, demonstrating as they do the simplicity and subtlety of his language. The small husband's caterpillar bitten hand is a superb image of innocence and nature's animalism. Because she feels guilty about having had sexual relations with Spotty Dog, Hsiao-hsiao attempts to soothe her husband's injury, an injury for which she assumes responsibility.

She tried everything she could think of to get rid of the thing in herself. Only her husband knew that her belly was getting big, but he didn't dare tell his parents. He had more love, and more fear, too, for her than for his parents.

She still remembered what had happened on the day that Spotty Dog took his oath. When autumn came, *more caterpillars appeared around the house.* The small husband often talked about how he had been bitten by one of them. It seemed that he intentionally mentioned this incident to torture her. It made her sad. She hated the caterpillars, and wanted to step on them whenever she saw them.[28] (italics mine)

In such a natural and delicate way, Shen Ts'ung-wen returns to the caterpillar, which represents both guilt and desire. It is another example of the author's fluid prose style, one which can dilate, or expand, omitting the ornate without, at the same time, omitting the ornament. It is one prose writer's poetry.

Her son married a girl six years older than he when he was twelve. . . . On his wedding day, Hsiao-hsiao was watching the gay bustle by the fence with the *elm* over it, holding her newly born baby, just as she had held her own husband ten years before.[29] (italics mine)

Finally, everything is resolved for Hsiao-hsiao. Like the bride in *The Lovers*, she remains intact and inviolate, even after insult, accusation, punishment and threats of death by drowning. The elm and the newly born baby hint at the natural life force, with which Hsiao-hsiao has affinity, and which keeps her intact, both as character, and in a larger sense, as human being. But the author's story is not complete—there is yet the marriage of Hsiao-hsiao's son to a girl several years his senior. It means that the human story is cyclical. Hsiao-hsiao is a better realized character than the country girl Ts'ui-ts'ui of *The Border Town*. Hsiao-hsiao, perhaps, is innocence incarnate, while Ts'ui-ts'ui on the other hand represents Shen Ts'ung-wen's ideal. The former is not perfect, but real—the latter is perfect, but not real.

Three Men and a Girl
(*Wild Blue Chrysanthemums in the Stone Cave*)

Three Men and a Girl is one of Shen Ts'ung-wen's best stories, superb in several different ways: in textural density; characterization; built-in, organic symbolism; and inviolable theme. The characterization in the story was discussed in the previous chapter. Now, we are concerned with theme, imagery, and style.

In the opening paragraphs of the story, the author writes about an army battalion marching in the rain to a new post.

We marched for four days until we reached the town. The weather was curious, for it turned fine at the moment we reached town. There might be some people who would laugh at this event, thinking the sun was shining only to harass us. We soldiers didn't mind. We had come to take over garrison duty in town. The former garrison had been moved, and we had come to fill the vacancy and continue all the nonsense that had once been their lot.[30]

This passage enhances the atmosphere of absurdity and boredom created by previous paragraphs about the rain. In addition, the passage also suggests the unpredictability of nature, and the inevitability of death. The author goes on to suggest what death is like. When the soldiers are camped in the temple and bugler blows a martial response on the stone lion in front of the temple, Shen Ts'ung-wen describes the scene as follows:

From the south end of the street came two stout dogs of neatly clipped fur and sly eyes, like two newly born babies standing before the people. These creatures must have sensed what was happening at the temple and come over for a look.

This monstrous pair lured us into an illusion. Our habit was that whenever we saw a fat dog, there immediately rose from our hearts an irrepressible urge to slaughter. But here was something more arresting: We heard a girl's voice calling "Ah-pai, Ah-pai," feeble, yet clear. The dogs looked at us for a while, as if understanding that they couldn't stay there long—then turned and ran away.[31]

The dogs are not obtrusive. Nor is the narrator's urge to slaughter. On a symbolic level, the dogs represent death—the beast. At the same time, the dogs are human and understanding. That is, the dogs are an ambivalent symbol; they represent both the beastliness of death and its attraction. As soon as the dogs hear the girl's "feeble" voice, they run off. Here, the girl's voice is an embodiment of love associated with death. Without overplaying his tone, without any overstatement, the author suggests the theme of his story: love and death.

The dogs refuse to eat the food offered by the two soldiers, but accept it from the young beancurd vendor.

In time, the two dogs became friendlier. Upon seeing us, they would come over cautiously to the beancurd shop. *We hated these creatures, yet liked them, too.* Even if we were getting along nicely, they would leave us when they heard the girl's voice calling from across the street.[32] (italics mine)

This passage contains the two soldiers' ambivalent attitude toward death. It is different from the shopkeeper's: he and the beasts are attracted to each other. And the beasts are associated with the girl. Thus, through the symbol of the dogs (death), the shopkeeper is associated with the girl. With utmost delicacy, the author moves the Countryman toward his doom; his union with death.

The girl came out of the door and stood there; the two big white dogs bounced up and down by her side, circling round her, then *licked her small hands with their darting red tongues.*[33] (italics mine)

Once more, the author's evocation of his tale's latent dark forces is flawless. Symbols abound, and they are unmistakably concrete: red tongues lapping at the small hands, dogs circling like vultures round the girl. While the scene and its implication of doom are not frightful, the touch of death is imminent. At the end of the story, the girl kills herself by swallowing several gold pieces. Her body disappears from its grave; and the shopkeeper disappears, too. "The body of the girl was discovered in a stone cave half a mile from the grave. It had been stripped; and littered about the floor surrounding it were wild blue chrysanthemums...."[34]

Stone cave, naked corpse, wild blue chrysanthemums: these are the natural symbols of the marriage between death and love in their natural forms.

CHAPTER 10

Censored and Silenced

AT the end of the Sino-Japanese War, Nationalist and Communist party representatives began their own peace negotiations. The Communists, in their expansionary drives, had taken over some provinces on the Nationalist periphery and were gradually gaining strength. Perhaps for this reason, the peace talks accomplished little. In December, 1948, the Communist army surrounded Peking. During the siege, and before the fall of the city, one of Shen Ts'ung-wen's students wrote to ask the writer's opinion of the political impasse. Shen replied:

The present government is corrupt and paralyzed in every respect and continues to be incorrigible. We writers of this age, the age beginning with the May Fourth uprising thirty years ago, have used our pens in the democratic and scientific spirit, and have toiled unselfishly. We have done our best, particularly in cultural areas. Our burgeoning society demands sacrifices from young stalwarts like you. Regardless of political fluctuations, the construction of a new country depends on honest and diligent youth. You ask what you, personally, can do to offset the status-quo . . . I can only remind you that it is futile to escape. Since we are here to stay, we have to dedicate ourselves to learning from our past mistakes. We can no longer afford to seek protection behind our old shield: we must stop being bookworms.[1]

Following the collapse of Peking on the first of February, 1949, written indictments began to appear on the walls of Peking University. Radical students called these walls, repositories of dissent, "Walls of Democracy." Along with scrawled condemnations of people and institutions considered undesirable by the radical students were anti-Shen Ts'ung-wen posters which labeled him "pink writer"—a derogatory appellation steeped in erotic allusions, authored by Kuo Mo-jo, one-time vice-chairman of the Standing Committee of the National

111

People's Congress. Other posters described Shen as a "prostitute writer" who refused to take sides and was of "regressive ideology." His mail was crammed with threats and intimidating sketches of bullets. The hate campaign was systematic, relentless. Even prior to Peking's fall, Shen had begun giving away books from his private library, saying, "Maybe I deserve interdiction. But these books are blameless. They shouldn't perish with me."[2]

After the siege came the occupation. An uneasy truce hung over Peking as she readied herself for another regime. Propagandists for the radical forces exhorted the Pekingese to "Welcome the Liberation Army," and "Extend Political Learning." This mood of collaboration displeased Shen, but he was exhausted and on the verge of a nervous breakdown. Resistance, of any kind, seemed foolhardy at the time, so he moved to the suburbs, grateful for a chance to rest in temporary quarters provided for him by Tsinghua University. Upon his recovery, he moved his family back to Peking. The situation there had not changed; the hate campaign was still in full sway. Political committees dispatched emissaries to "counsel" Shen and to "cleanse" his thoughts. Soon, it was rumored in dormitories and cafeterias of Peking University that Shen Ts'ung-wen had tried to commit suicide and failed. Ma Feng-hua, one of his former students and an assistant professor in the Department of Economics at the University of Washington, wrote in the spring of 1953:

Afterwards, when I went to the Shen residence to check on the story, I learned that Mr. Shen had swallowed some kerosene, and cut his throat and wrists with sharp blades. Miraculously, he survived these wounds. For several days he lay comatose in a small clinic. . . . When I saw Mrs. Shen, she looked pale, and she said, "It's better for us not to see him now. Let him rest for a while." Such was his emotional state that Mr. Shen mistook his sick-ward for a prison. After regaining perspective, he wrote vigorously in bed, then pleaded with his wife to fetch Mr. Yang Jun-t'ung so he could be rescued.

Following his nightmarish experience in the hospital, Mr. Shen was in extremely bad health. On my visit once, his face and eyes were swollen and blood kept oozing from his nostrils. So profoundly depressed was he that he blurted out to me, "How can I understand? Those aristocratic writers grew up in green-houses during their adolescence; they had money to study abroad. They may have contributed to society then; today, they fuss over some bureaucrat's birthday feast; tomorrow, they will attend another V.I.P. party. All this, since the Communist take-over. I come from peasant stock. I was an army private for years. Granted that my political indoctrination in the past was limited, and that I have lagged behind in that regard up to now . . . still, why am I not given an opportunity to rejoin the team? What specifically have I done? What have the Communists in store for me? If they'd only specify what they want. . . . I might make the effort. Death doesn't frighten me. Why this campaign of vilification toward me personally? I am not without friends in the Communist fold: there is Ting Ling, for one, and a lot of former students . . . Ho Ch'i-fang,[3] for instance. Let them come and tell me just what exactly the Communists think of me. But I am allowed to see no one.[4]

Partially recovered, and somewhat reluctantly reinstated in the university through the efforts of unknown parties, Shen learned that this new arrangement was tenuous, since his course in the Chinese Department at Peking University had been cancelled. His demotion took an ironic turn when he was assigned as a minor employee in the Museum of Peking where his main responsibility was to label antiques. It appeared that the new regime was determined to hold him incommunicado, at least for the time being.

Before long, Mrs. Shen began to attend classes at the University of North China. She had become a friend of the organization—a necessary step before attaining party membership. The two Shen children were themselves conscripts in the Youth Corps and the Children Teams in school (Communist Youth organizations designed to facilitate political indoctrination and campaigns). Only the head of the family remained comparatively obscure in this political "assimilation." Ma Feng-hua describes Shen's discomfiture at this time:

This period seemed to be most trying for Mr. Shen. With his wife residing at the University of North China, Mr. Shen languished in the museum, spending long hours in self-evaluation. In the evening, he had to feed the children, tuck them in bed. Only when the housework was done could he permit himself the luxury of solitude. He stayed up late, listening to classical music. One night, as I sat with him listening to the classics, he said, as though in a trance, "My brain has gone completely fallow. Music remains the sole stimulus

for my imagination. Sometimes I have the sensation that I am
back in the countryside of Hunan. I hear the flowing of a small river;
I smell the green grass; I catch the trembling sound of cricket wings
in my ears. . . . Only at such moments do I regain that spark of
creativity. Yet, what I write feverishly at night, I almost maniacally
tear up in the morning."[5]

Around autumn, 1950, Shen Ts'ung-wen, with some misgivings,
enrolled in the Political Research Institute of the People's Revolutionary University for orientation courses. He tried to meet
the new regime halfway; his reward—barely passing marks. The
inquisition was far from over. In 1951, Ting Ling won second
prize in the Stalin Literary Awards for her *The Sun Shines
Over the Sangkan River*. She asked Shen to contribute to the
magazine *People's Literature*. His answer: "I have lost contact
with the new literary periodicals. It would be better if you
were to give me two readable articles so I'll know what to write."
Ting Ling obliged. Shen's essay, *My Learning*, was serialized
in the November 19-21, 1951 editions of *Ta-kung Pao*, published
in Hong Kong.

My Learning is full of self-reproach and appraisal of the
success of the Communist Party in China. Shen's major concern
is to emphasize his past life as a soldier and his refusal to embrace current political struggles which the Communist party
considers an error—because to the party, "politics is above everything," and "everything should follow politics," "literature and
arts should follow politics, to serve the good of the masses":

In the past twenty years, I have not understood thoroughly the
essence of literature. That's why I have, whenever I have touched
upon literature, art, and politics, taken the liberal attitude of an
old intellectual, thinking that it is impossible, unnecessary, and
erroneous for literature to be attached to politics. And I thought that
one must struggle for the freedom to doubt and negate despotic
regimes, so as to attain a healthier development and progress as a
writer. I used my pen in such a manner that even though I did not
compromise with traditional politics, I gradually drifted from the
demands of the people's revolution. I have written quite a lot these
twenty years, and I have made many mistakes.[6]

Shen said his understanding of politics was affected by history. In the past, politics had meant to him despotism because

he had seen a great deal of cruelty, bribery, and bureaucracy during the time of the warlords. The politics he understood before he was twenty both terrified and annoyed him. He admitted:

On the one hand, I did not understand the significance in the current literary movement of "politics above everything" to the people's revolution; on the other hand, I admitted that the progressive social ideal of "for all and by all" was at the same time philosophy and poetry. In one respect, I was in despair for politics; in another, I knew little and connected little with the struggles for a new reality. Thus, my work was gradually isolated from the mass of people, and from the shifting demand of social reform. Especially in my writing, I overlooked essence and emphasized form. For the past twenty years, I have been the unknowing tool of intellectuals of the old society, and pseudo-liberalists. My works was of no use to the people's revolution, and it benefited the unbroken feudal rule of the old Nationalist Party. From September 19, 1931 (the Mukden Incident), professors among the old intellectuals have been selling themselves to the Big Rice Ball clique of the Four Big Families.[7] This group of professors decorated the eve of the collapse of the Big Rice Ball political clique. Due to my concern for social convention, my behavior abetted this small group of scum, and was harmful to the people's revolution.[8]

Shen was particularly critical of his own writing:

After 1928, my life was spent in schools and happened to have stronger ties to intellectuals of the Anglo-American school who were battling for democracy and freedom. Although my work habits remained the same, my way of life gradually changed and I became a half-intellectual. In one respect, my contact with society did not extend beyond students and colleagues: in another, the scope of my reading became more diffused. Then, I was an energetic and prolific writer, about to help establish a new publishing enterprise. Readers were to be found not only in schools, but as members of other modern enterprises. My work received encouragement and stimulation; I became an intimate member of the short story writer group. Most of my work had been produced within the previous twenty year period. Some of this was comparably progressive, but some reflected a weakness of the wandering intellectual: my language was flowery, but my thoughts were confused; I had a style but no sense of life. Most of my writing was of no use to the people's revolution. It had a detrimental effect on youth, and it numbed their will to progress. The stories I wrote that I had adapted from the Buddhist classics reveal the mixture of my encyclopedic learning. I confused the nihilism of Buddhism with my exotic feelings, and the various studies of the anthologies of the Spring and Autumn Era scholars with which I was familiar. The confusion produced very sick, paganistic, and unhealthy books like *The Seven Color Nightmare*. Works which stimulated my development obviously included the writings of Freud and Joyce, whose incomplete and shattered reflections could be seen in my own work.[9]

Saying that he had a better and more thorough understanding of "collectivism," Shen Ts'ung-wen ended his essay by praising what he had learned from the new age, and emphasizing the depth of his feeling for the birth of a new China. Probably because he was considered to have satisfactorily reformed his ideological point of view, Shen was released after ten months from the Political Research Institute of the People's Revolutionary University. He returned to his old job at the Museum of Peking.

In February, 1956, at the Twentieth Grand Conference of the Communist party, Shen Ts'ung-wen delivered this apologia:

I am an old cog in the intelligentsia. These past years I have made writing my career. My origins are rural. Because of the modest success I had as a writer, I became conceited, aloof, not unlike an uncooperative peasant who never participates in any civic function and is therefore impervious to all human endeavor. As a result, my thinking was gradually corrupted, then enslaved by the semi-colonialized bourgeoisie. Consequently, the general direction of my work became increasingly detestable, seducing young readers—luring them into escapism and lulling them into a false sense of security, even in their static condition. I adhered stubbornly to a hypocritical liberalism. My excuse was that I could never become a dupe of Chiang Kai-shek's venal administration. This was self-deception, of course. With no proper affiliations, without a reliable background, I was incapable of distinguishing the dangerous trends in the enemy's published works. This oversight enhanced Chiang Kai-shek's reign: worse, it was detrimental to the welfare of the people. Then came the liberation of Peking; it was my salvation. I was spared the fate of becoming just another mindless hack.

After the liberation, I turned to the study of antiques. Even with the help and encouragement of the Party's long-term indoctrination, which entails service to the populace in the field of technical arts development, many problems have arisen. As my ideological standards are inferior, my credentials in historical studies insufficient, and since that old peasant uncooperativeness in me has not been completely purged, my present work is erratic and cannot bear close scrutiny. Whatever I have achieved is not commensurate with the requisites of society....

In the past thirty years, I did not believe it possible that any political party could make China prosper. Despotic as Chiang Kai-shek's rule was, and even though I myself had predicted its demise, I had never seriously considered and analyzed which political structure could best replace it. Such redemptive measures as "People's Liberation," and "Reform of Individualism" were frankly incomprehensible to me....[10]

The speech went on to catalogue the numerous achievements of the new regime. In conclusion, Shen said, "I believe in the Communist Party. I must get abreast of its more distinguished exponents; I must invigorate myself with Marxism-Leninism through the writings of Chairman Mao.... I must plumb the very depths of my soul, and try my best to become a new intellectual in Mao Tse-tung's time. I will avail myself of all practical knowledge and offer its fruits to my country.... I will try to redeem the pen I exploited and abandoned for so long that I may praise this new age, this new country, this new people."[11]

Shen was careful not to show any of the qualms he must have felt for his public apology. Like it or not, he had been chosen as a "showpiece" and as such was subject to the public's charity or scorn. It had been eight years since Shen Ts'ung-wen had published any creative work. Persecution, coercion, public denunciation—these were but small efforts on the part of the Communists who were determined to subjugate completely the practicing artist. Either due to his public self-flagellation, or because the Communist party deemed him sufficiently rehabilitated (especially after the publication of *Designs in Chinese Silk and Linen,* a collection of reproductions from the Warring Kingdoms era to the Ch'ing Dynasty, co-authored by Shen and Wang Chia-shu), the errant writer was permitted to publish *Selected Stories of Shen Ts'ung-wen,* courtesy of *People's Litera-*

ture. Even then, many of the stories in the collection were drastically revised, not only to get them past the censors, but to update the author's sagging popularity. To one long accustomed to being his own boss where creative work was concerned, having been saddled overnight with a rubber-stamp editor must have recalled for Shen his youthful experiences as whipping boy on various army posts. Superficially, the changes were minimal; what could not easily be borne was that with some incidental doctoring here and there, the authorial voice, if not the literary style, was altered beyond credibility. Consider *Existence,* a short story Shen wrote in 1936. It deals with a young man's struggle to eke out a living as an artist and as an individual after moving to Peking from his hometown. In one powerful scene, we see him crazed with hunger. Pride makes him take a walk in order not to be around when the other tenants in his rooming house prepare to eat their supper. He wanders aimlessly down dark streets, his mind fastened on thoughts of his ailing wife. As rewritten by Communist editors, the same section appeared thusly: He had a wife with whom he taught at a primary school. *Since she had not participated in Nationalist Party functions, her old position had been pre-empted by someone else.* Jobless and bedridden with tuberculosis, she was at present living with her father. He had not heard from her lately.[12] The italicized line is courtesy of the new regime. In this way, the Nationalist party was denounced for corruption, and the implication that the party was responsible for unemployment and ill-health underscored.

The Mountain Passer (1934) indicates in its original version those parts excised, this time, by the Nationalist government. The story recounts the mission and death of a young *messenger* (new version) or a *spy* (revised original), during the Nationalist-Communist war. The young messenger is assigned to deliver secret radio dispatches to his compatriots up in the mountains. En route he sees a cuckoo flying overhead, which "seemed to know the secret in the bamboo bushes, and flew away at once." The courier curses: "You *** very smart! You can go to *** and become a spy...."[13]

The missing words, represented by asterisks, referred to the Nationalists. Since that line of dialogue contained an obscenity directed at the government then in power, it was deleted. Shen Ts'ung-wen very shrewdly left in all the asterisks. Other parts of the first version of the story were so extensively edited that the syntactical structure of the revision bordered on unintelligibility. In the new version (1957), the obscenity spoken by the young man is lovingly spelled out: "You *mother-fucker*, very smart! You can go to Nanking to become a spy and receive a salary of $250 a month!"[14]

The new revision, as might be expected, was loaded with propaganda. First, it romanticized the Communist credo as represented by the messenger: to serve and die as an "agent" in the Communist army was an honor; whereas being a "spy" in Nanking simply meant turning into a mercenary, a cheap one at that—$250 a month. Altruism and fortitude then, according to this one-sided assessment, were strictly Communist attributes and were not to be found among Nationalist "spies" who were doomed to corruption.

In *The Mountain Passer,* nine of the original twenty messengers laid down their lives before the hero himself was killed; raw recruits were left to carry on the good fight.

An excerpt, from the Nationalist version: "thus, there has been a step-up in the workload, with its responsibilities delegated to an overworked few—without any explanation. However, this is * * *, everyone must bite his lips *** in silence."[15] The same excerpt, from the Communist version: "however, this is revolution! It is cruel struggle! Everyone must bite his lips, grind his teeth, endure in silence, and wait for the chance to counter-attack!"[16]

Designs in Chinese Silk and Linen and *The Selected Stories of Shen Ts'ung-wen* were followed by the publication in November, 1958 of *Bronze Mirrors of the T'ang and Sung Dynasties.* The book carried lithographs of mirror designs ranging from the era of the Warring Kingdoms, to the T'ang, Sung, and Ch'ing dynasties, with special emphasis on reproductions of T'ang and Sung mirrors.

Shen's museum job was not altogether a waste of time and effort. The research work served as a kind of buffer to politics. Besides, Shen had been exposed to cultural artifacts during one of his army stints, and he had not lost his fascination with antiquity. Quite a few essayists had built a camouflage of political immunity about them by resorting to secondary occupations, such as doing annotations for scholarly journals and writing introductions to classics. Shen was practically the museum's curator. As early as 1936, in *Housewife*, an autobiographical story celebrating his marriage, the one-time army clerk had written about his love of antiques. The young bride in the story says: "You like to fondle those brittle things. It's not enough that you must spend your money on them; you expect friends to buy them for you as gifts. How strange."[17] To which the husband replies: "It's not strange at all. It's my hobby. Do you like these green flower vases?" He goes on to romanticize: "One should have a hobby; although once it's there, it can easily become an addiction. I don't have the cash to collect bronze or jade; I don't have the eye to collect scriptures and scrolls. What I do collect are inexpensive objects, and they are not without value."[18]

Shen's profile of this mercurial collector is as luminous and varicolored as carnival fare:

He has too much iron in his blood, too much imagination, too many wayward habits. To him society is both school and family. Clever yet naïve, passionate without being demonstrative, he is desirous of achievment but has no industry for it. He is an astute observer of human behavior but is not a good mixer. While he loves his wife, he is incapable of flattery or amorous attention. He is consistently himself, therefore irresponsible. This is what offends his wife most—his receptivity which is flawed by its romanticism. Being the way he is, his gratifications are narrow and do not include his family. He is not without self-knowledge; in his bachelor days, he was well aware of his personal shortcomings and was determined to correct them after marriage so that he might become one in the emotional partnership the institution demands. He has long realized that in order to facilitate this, he must first subordinate his innermost self. . . . He knows that any hobby . . . becomes finally obsessive. . . . Ironically, his passion for inexpensive objects is not selfishly motivated. Through these objects he hopes to endow his family with a touch of culture and a bit of harmony.[19]

In retrospect, *Housewife* impresses us with its derisive ironies. Between fact and fiction, between the collector and literary creator, the reader is tempted to make loose connections that may in fact not exist. Have we not all, at one time or another, been tempted to identify an author and his circumstances with the cast and events he writes about in stories we assume to be autobiographical? And if these factual and fictional circumstances match, however circumstantially, do we not feel vindicated? *Housewife,* however, was not a piece of factual autobiographical writing as we typically think of it; and Shen's museum job was not a surrender to his hobby. It was a shield. If his wife and children had to make concessions to the Communists, the question of "unpracticality" is academic.

In December, 1961, Shen Ts'ung-wen, along with nine others in a touring group sponsored by the Chinese Writers' Union, traveled to Ching-kang Mountain in Kiangsi, scene of the Red Army's initial growth during the late twenties. On this trip, Shen wrote five poems in one of the classical verse forms—rhymed verse, with each line having five characters. Published in the spring of 1962, these poems are rather subdued in their inventory of the new China when compared to the more saccharine works of his fellow tourists.

An example of Shen's latest work:

> Now with white hair, I learn even to write poetry;
> Reviewing the past, I sing of the present.
>> from "Down the Mountain Path on
>> the Way Back to Nan-ch'ang"[20]

Shen's tone now is less of praise than of nostalgia. In *Festival and Lanterns,* a collection of essays printed in 1963, Shen again echoes the theme of nostalgia and mourns the decline of the agricultural past in the reconstruction of the state. Relics of that bygone age are votive lanterns still featured in New Class festivities. Shen cites a poem from the Sung Dynasty about a troupe dancer:

The episode transpired on a New Year's Eve eight hundred years ago: a young girl from a small dance troupe returns home in the middle of the night and comes upon lanterns burning low. The reflection and reverberations of this story I caught a century later . . . by the same token, after eight hundred years, with three centuries of the Yüan, Ming and Ch'ing Dynasties, there has not been any considerable reform. The only identifiable changes are those manifest in political parties.

Ten years after the Liberation, these changes have become fundamental. My childhood experiences are now regarded as anachronisms —the rural past. Even today, it is not inconceivable that young men with backgrounds similar to mine are experiencing what I did when I was their age, although with a marked difference. On the other hand, other young men reared and educated in the cities have no inkling of what that other life is like.[21]

In each of the essays in *Festivals and Lanterns* Shen addresses himself to the passing of China's agrarian traditions. His literary style here, as of old, is fresh and rhythmical; his critical stance is firm. But it is his enchantment with nonindustrialized, noncollectivized eras that undermines his chances of ever becoming one of the molders of his country's future shape. He is a Countryman by temperament and has no place in a culture whose restive millions are dreaming of their own industrial age.

There is no record of any new fiction by Shen Ts'ung-wen after the Communist takeover of Mainland China in 1949. Now sixty-nine years old, he stands on the brink of literary eradication. As he admitted in *Festivals and Lanterns* (1963), his "memories are gradually fading...." As far as the rest of the world is concerned, he is in limbo. A passage from *The Diary of The Non-dead* (1928) foreshadowed his present condition: "As for literature, I have come into troubled times... I should bind my hands...."[22]

Figuratively—and perhaps even literally—he has done just that. His self-abnegation gives credence to Lu Hsün's words: "Most people believe the sword is used only to command soldiers. They do not realize that it can also be used to humble men of letters."[23]

Shen Ts'ung-wen, writer and scholar, lives the lonely life of an exile in his own country. He has been cut off from his friends, his peers, and the masses who stand to gain from his unexpurgated work. His tragedy—which is the state's triumph—widens the gulf between two ideologies. And contemporary literature is one culture poorer for having been shut off from an essentially fertile source.

CHAPTER 11

Conclusion

THE stories discussed in this book are among Shen Ts'ung-wen's best. He has written many others that merit discussion, such as *The Husband, Living, Night, The Inn, Kuei-sheng, A Scene in Kuei-chou, The Housewife, San-san, Big and Small Yüan*, to name only a few. Limitation of space makes a lengthy discussion impossible. I would, however, like to mention other works that illustrate the variety of Shen Ts'ung-wen's themes, narrative style, and characters: for instance, *Scenes Under the Moon*, a group of fables based on Buddhist tales; *The Witch Doctor's Love*, a novelette about China's aboriginal tribes; *Alice in China*, a novel after the manner of *Alice's Adventures in Wonderland*. The short story, though, is Shen Ts'ung-wen's strongest form. In his preface to *Alice in China*, he admits the failure of his book: "I didn't succeed in my satire about social ills buried in amusing innocence... didn't make (my satire) clear or natural enough. And it sounds superficial when it is most painstakingly satirical...."[1] Su Hsüeh-lin, another contemporary, criticized *The Witch Doctor's Love* in her article "On Shen Ts'ung-wen": "The story is romantic; the description is pure imagination; the dialogue is westernized and doesn't sound like anything from the simple aborigines.... The aborigines' songs, for instance, sound like Western love songs...."[2] The remarks made both by Shen Ts'ung-wen and Su Hsueh-lin are justified.

Even as a short-fiction writer, Shen Ts'ung-wen is not as flawless as one might wish. His preference for the "plain narrative" exposes him to criticism—sometimes deservedly—as a loose writer, and a writer with "structural deficiencies." Perhaps in his own defense, he wrote in his epilogue to *Pebble Ferry*:

123

From this small collection, one may conclude that my approach to fiction is closer to essay writing. Although essay writing is also frequently exhaustively descriptive, little stress is put on structure. Ingredients traditionally indispensable to short story writing, such as "denouement," "suspense," and "climax" do not interest me in the least. I write plainly as I see it; my material dictates its own style, and the style drives to a resolution of material. . . . The event I choose may be commonplace, trivial; it does not matter. There is no exaggeration, and the piece is written straight through without cutting or trimming. I have not as yet written anything that people could rightly call a "story" in the traditional sense. I would rather fail out of the technical limits of fiction than succeed within them.[3]

Contemporary critical estimations of Shen Ts'ung-wen's literary merits and demerits point out, somewhat snobbishly, that he is a rough diamond among supposedly more polished gems. To those critics, the rough gem metaphor means that Shen Ts'ung-wen is a "realist" or a "naturalist." They ignore him as a symbolist. They also ignore him as a writer whose Countryman foreshadowed the appearance in literature of a modern alienated man. Not only does Shen's Countryman transcend his origins, he becomes a raceless character, and therefore a timeless character. It would be an injustice to arrive at any literary evaluation of Shen Ts'ung-wen's writing on the basis of his early works, which admittedly lack craftsmanship. His more successful stories, nonetheless, will stand careful critical scrutiny. They are, in Shen Ts'ung-wen's own words, structured so that they "converge to become abysses and extend to become lakes."

Notes and References

Chapter One

1. Miao is one of the 345 tribes who inhabit the southwest and west of China. The Miaos live mostly in Yünnan and West Hunan Provinces, and have been considered by some to be one of the folk groups of the T'ai people. See: T. R. Tregear, *A Geography of China* (Chicago: Aldine, 1965), pp. 62-63.

2. Ch'en Brook and Mayang are both tributaries of the River Yüan. The boats that sail these tributaries bear their names.

3. Shen Ts'ung-wen, *Autobiography of Ts'ung-wen* (Hong Kong: Wen-li, 1960), pp. 11-12.

4. Shen Ts'ung-wen, *Letters Saved from Oblivion* (Kunming: K'ai-ming Press, 1943), pp. 33-34.

5. Shen Ts'ung-wen, *Autobiography of Ts'ung-wen*, pp. 21-22.

Chapter Two

1. Shen Ts'ung-wen, *Autobiography of Ts'ung-wen*, pp. 26-31.

2. Yüan Shih-k'ai, a northern warlord represented the feudal-comprador government after the 1911 Revolution. In 1916, an abortive attempt to restore the monarchy led to Yüan's downfall. He died in the same year.

3. In 1900, there broke out a vast and spontaneous movement, the Yi-ho-tuan (Boxer) Movement. Forming themselves into secret societies based on superstitious cults, these peasants and handicrafts-men of North China carried on an armed struggle against foreign invaders. The joint forces of the eight imperialist powers: Britain, the United States, Japan, Germany, Tsarist Russia, France, Italy, and Austria occupied Peking and Tientsin and suppressed the movement. The Manchu government was eventually compelled to sign the Protocol of 1901.

4. *Autobiography of Ts'ung-wen*, pp. 70-71.

5. *Ibid.*, p. 74.

Chapter Three

1. *Autobiography of Ts'ung-wen*, p. 113.

2. Part of a system of Hindu logic, rather like syllogism.

3. The major form of Buddhism in China. The idea is to devote one's whole self to the transcendence of all flesh, rather than to strive for Nirvana, as in Hsiu-cheng. Ta-cheng, in Sanskrit, is *mahayana.*

4. *Autobiography of Ts'ung-wen,* p. 136.

5. A Hunan governor-general in the Ch'ing government who ruled during the 1860's in China. His talents as militiaman and as army officer have been greatly admired.

6. See Chapter 4, this book, p. 38.

7. *Autobiography of Ts'ung-wen,* pp. 140-41.

Chapter Four

1. Ts'ao Chü-jen, *Fifty Years of the Literary Scene* (Wen-t'an wu-shih nien), (Hong Kong: New Culture, 1969), p. 43.

2. Chow Tse-tsung, *The May Fourth Movement* (Stanford: Stanford University Press, 1967), p. 10.

3. Tibor Mende, *The Chinese Revolution* (London: Thames and Hudson, 1961), p. 50.

4. Teng Ssu-yu and John K. Fairbank, *China's Response to the West: A Documentary Study 1893-1923* (Cambridge: Harvard Univ. Press, 1966), p. 239.

5. *Ibid.,* p. 240.

6. *The May Fourth Movement,* pp. 300-303.

7. Ch'en Tu-hsiu, *Collected Works of Tu-hsiu* (Tu-hsiu wen-ts'un), (Shanghai: Ya-tung, 1922), p. 362.

8. *Ibid.,* p. 362.

9. *China's Response to the West,* p. 239.

Chapter Five

1. Ting Ling, born 1904. She won the Stalin Prize for Literature in 1951. A close friend of Shen Ts'ung-wen's, she was converted to Marxism in 1931 after the death of her husband, Hu Yeh-p'in, a young poet. In 1957, she was expelled from the Chinese Communist party as a rightist. It was reported that in 1958, Ting Ling was working as a charwoman in the Peking headquarters of the Writers' Association. Ting Ling was a well-known literary figure in China for about thirty years.

2. Hu Yeh-p'in (1907-31), a young poet and ardent Communist who worked for the League of Left-Wing Writers in China in the late 1920's. He was arrested and executed by the Nationalists in Shanghai. He was known as one of the five martyrs of the League of Left-Wing Writers.

3. The Kuomintang regime began a purge campaign from 1927 to 1930 before the outbreak of the War of Resistance against Japan. The group attacked the Communist-led trade unions, closing them and driving them underground. All activities of the workers and their leaders were suppressed. About 80 percent of those who were engaged in the struggle were either fired or killed.

4. The Northern Expedition Army led by the Kuomintang and National Government under Chiang Kai-shek in the south of China started its northward march in July, 1926. With the support of the majority of the local population, the Northern Expedition Army advanced victoriously, defeating the imperialist supported Northern warlords. By January of 1927, the expedition had achieved a degree of independence and unification for China.

Chapter Six

1. Shen Ts'ung-wen, *In Reminiscence of Hu Yeh-p'in* (Shanghai: Kwang-hua, 1932), p. 62.

2. *Ibid.*, pp. 62-63.

3. Shen Ts'ung-wen, *In Reminiscence of Ting Ling* (Shanghai: Liang-yu, 1934), pp. 165-68.

Chapter Seven

1. Wen Tzu-ch'uan, ed., *Selected Stories and Essays of Shen Ts'ung-wen* (Hong Kong: New Learning, 1957), pp. 1-2.

2. *Ibid.*, p. 3.

3. Ting Ling, "The Life of an Honest Man," preface to *Selected Works of Hu Yeh-p'in* (Kunming: K'ai-ming, 1951), p. 17.

4. Shen Ts'ung-wen, *In Reminiscence of Hu Yeh-p'in*, p .78.

5. Shen Ts'ung-wen, *The Border Town* (Kunming: K'ai-ming, 1943), p. 1.

6. Shen Ts'ung-wen, *In Reminiscence of Ting Ling, Continued* (Shanghai: Liang-yu, 1939), p. 137.

7. Wen Tzu-ch'uan, ed., *Selected Stories and Essays of Shen Ts'ung-wen*, p. 92.

8. *Ibid.*, p. 94.

9. Liang Shih-ch'iu, *Random Talks on Hsü Chih-mo* (Taiwan: Far Eastern Book Co., 1958), p. 2.

10. Shen Ts'ung-wen, *Ah-chin* (Kunming: K'ai-ming, 1943), pp. 8-9.

11. Tibor Mende, *The Chinese Revolution*, p. 129.

12. *Selected Stories and Essays of Shen Ts'ung-wen*, pp. 94-95.

13. *Ibid.*, p. 99.

Chapter Eight

1. Shen Ts'ung-wen, *Exercise*, Preface to *Ah-chin*, pp. 3-4.

2. Shen Ts'ung-wen, *Box Cliff*, in *Random Sketches on a Trip to West Hunan* (Kunming: K'ai-ming, 1943), p. 73.

3. Shen Ts'ung-wen, *Three Men and a Girl* in *The New and the Old* (Kunming: Liang-yu, 1944), p. 42.

4. *Ibid.*, p. 45.

5. *Ibid.*, p. 52.

6. *Ibid.*, p. 53.

7. *Ibid.*, pp. 53-55.

8. *Ibid.*, p. 60.

9. Shen Ts'ung-wen, *Construction*, in *The Collected Works of Shen Ts'ung-wen* (Shanghai: Crescent Moon, 1931), p. 148.

10. *Ibid.*, p. 146.

11. *Ibid.*, pp. 150-51.

12. *Ibid.*, p. 154.

13. *Ibid.*, pp. 165-66.

14. *Ibid.*, p. 168.

15. *Ibid.*, pp. 170-71.

16. *Ibid.*, p. 177.

17. *Ibid.*, p. 179.

18. *Ibid.*, p. 188.

19. Ho Yü-po, *Criticisms on Modern Chinese Writers* (Shanghai: Kwang-hua, 1932), p. 142.

20. Shen Ts'ung-wen, *Hui Ming*, in *Black Night* (Hong Kong: Wen-li, 1960), p. 1.

21. *Ibid.*, pp. 3-4.

22. C. T. Hsia, *A History of Modern Chinese Fiction* (New Haven: Yale Univ. Press, 1961), pp. 199-220.

23. Shen Ts'ung-wen, *Hui Ming*, p. 5.

24. *Ibid.*, p. 5.

25. *Ibid.*, p. 13.

26. *A History of Modern Chinese Fiction*, pp. 200-201.

27. *Hui Ming*, p. 16.

28. Shen Ts'ung-wen, "The New and the Old," in *The New and the Old* (Kunming: Liang-yu, 1944), p. 92.

29. *Ibid.*, p. 100.

30. Han Shih-heng, "Mr. Shen Ts'ung-wen's Fiction," in *Selected Essays of Literary Criticism* (Shanghai: Modern Press, 1934), p. 93.

31. Shen Ts'ung-wen, "To a Poet," in *Letters Saved from Oblivion,* p. 9.

32. Shen Ts'ung-wen, *Eight Steeds,* in *Spring and Lamp* (Hong Kong: Wen-li, 1960), p. 57.

33. *Ibid.,* pp. 58-59.

34. *Ibid.,* pp. 60-61.

35. *Ibid.,* p. 80.

36. *Ibid.,* p. 72.

37. Shen Ts'ung-wen, *The Border Town,* p. 7. (based on a translation of *The Chinese Earth,* by Ching Ti and Robert Payne, London: George Allen and Unwin, Ltd., 1947.)

38. *Ibid.,* pp. 8 and 11.

39. *Ibid.,* pp. 31-32.

40. *Exercise,* p. 6.

41. Shen Ts'ung-wen, "Preface to *The Border Town,*" in *The Border Town,* p. 3.

42. Shen Ts'ung-wen, *Mire,* in *Black Night,* pp. 72-73.

43. *Ibid.,* p. 74.

44. *Ibid.,* p. 76.

Chapter Nine

1. D. H. Lawrence, *Apocalypse* (New York: Viking, 1966), p. 200.

2. Su Hsueh-lin, *On Shen Ts'ung-wen,* from the Preface to *The Selected Works of Shen Ts'ung-wen* (Shanghai: Wan-hsiang, 1936), pp. 12-13.

3. Shen Ts'ung-wen, *Exercise of Emotions,* in *Letters Saved from Oblivion,* pp. 41-43.

4. "Exercise," pp. 5-7.

5. Shen Ts'ung-wen, *The Lovers,* in *Eight Steeds* (Hong Kong: Jih-hsin Book Co., 1960), p. 13.

6. *Ibid.,* p. 14.

7. *Ibid.,* pp. 14-15.

8. *Ibid.,* p. 15.

9. *Ibid.,* pp. 15-16.

10. *Ibid.,* p. 17.

11. *Ibid.,* p. 22.

12. *Ibid.,* p. 23.

13. Shen Ts'ung-wen, *A Passionate Boatman and a Passionate Woman,* in *Random Sketches on a Trip to West Hunan,* pp. 47-48.

14. Shen Ts'ung-wen, *Po-tzu,* in *Ah-chin,* pp. 50-51.

15. *Ibid.,* pp. 53-54.

16. *Ibid.,* p. 55.

17. *Ibid.*, p. 56.
18. *Ibid.*, p. 56.
19. *Ibid.*, pp. 56-57.
20. Shen Ts'ung-wen, *My Writing and the Waters,* in *Letters Saved from Oblivion,* p. 34.
21. *Po-tzu,* p. 58.
22. *Ibid.*, p. 60.
23. Shen Ts'ung-wen, *Quiet,* in *Black Phoenix* (Kunming: K'ai-ming, 1943), p. 43.
24. *Ibid.*, pp. 44-45.
25. *Ibid.*, p. 49.
26. Shen Ts'ung-wen, *Hsiao-hsiao,* in *The New and the Old,* p. 13.
27. *Ibid.*, p. 15.
28. *Ibid.*, pp. 18-19.
29. *Ibid.*, p. 21.
30. *Ibid.*, p. 43.
31. *Ibid.*, pp. 45-46.
32. *Ibid.*, p. 53.
33. *Ibid.*, p. 60.
34. *Ibid.*, p. 74.

Chapter Ten

1. Ma Feng-hua, *In Reminiscence of Professor Shen Ts'ung-wen, Biographical Literature,* II, no. 1 (year unknown), p. 13.
2. *Ibid.*, p. 13.
3. Ho Chi-fang, born 1912, poet and critic. He served as chairman of the Research Center of Literature in the Institute of Science in China.
4. Ma Feng-hua, *In Reminiscence of Professor Shen Ts'ung-wen,* p. 14.
5. *Ibid.*, p. 15.
6. Shen Ts'ung-wen, *My Learning* (Hong Kong: *Ta-kung Pao,* 19-22 November, 1951).
7. Four large families that once controlled the economic, political, and military power in Nationalist China: the Ch'ens, Chiangs, K'ungs, and Sungs.
8. *My Learning.*
9. *Ibid.*, November 21, 1951.
10. *Speech Given by Shen Ts'ung-wen.*
11. *Ibid.*
12. Shen Ts'ung-wen, *The Selected Works of Shen Ts'ung-wen* (Peking: People's Literature Press, 1957), p. 356.

13. Shen Ts'ung-wen, *Mountain Passer* (*Morning Light Literature Series*, 1934), p. 2. (Other publication data unavailable.)

14. *The Selected Works of Shen Ts'ung-wen*, p. 313.

15. *Mountain Passer*, p. 3.

16. *The Selected Works of Shen Ts'ung-wen*, p. 313.

17. Shen Ts'ung-wen, *Housewife* (Hong Kong: *Ming Pao Monthly*), I, no. 8, 1966, p. 54.

18. *Ibid.*, p. 54.

19. *Ibid.*, p. 56.

20. Shen Ts'ung-wen, *Morning on the Ching-kang Mountain* (Peking: *People's Literature*), February, 1962, p. 15. (Other publication data unavailable.)

21. Shen Ts'ung-wen, *Festivals and Lanterns* (Peking: *People's Literature*), April, 1963, p. 47. (Other publication data unavailable.)

22. Shen Ts'ung-wen, *The Diary of the Non-dead* (Shanghai: Human World, 1929), p. 63.

23. K. E. Priestly, ed., *China's Men of Letters* (Hong Kong: Dragonfly, 1962), p. 1.

Chapter Eleven

1. Shen Ts'ung-wen, *Aftermath*, in *Alice in China* (Shanghai: Crescent Moon, 1928), p. 2.

2. Su Hsüeh-lin, *On Shen Ts'ung-wen*, pp. 4-5.

3. Shen Ts'ung-wen, *Postface*, in *Pebble Ferry* (Shanghai: Chunghua, 1931), pp. 141-42.

4. *Exercise of Emotions*, p. 41.

Selected Bibliography

PRIMARY SOURCES
(In Chinese)

1. Fiction

Ah-chin. Kunming: K'ai-ming Press, 1943.
After Rain and Others. Shanghai: Spring Tide Press, 1928.
Alice in China. Shanghai: Crescent Moon Press, 1928.
Black Night. Hong Kong: Wen-li Press, 1960.
Black Phoenix. Kunming: K'ai-ming Press, 1943.
The Border Town. Kunming: K'ai-ming Press, 1943.
The Collected Works of Shen Ts'ung-wen: Chia. Shanghai: Kuo-kuang Press, 1930.
The Collected Works of Shen Ts'ung-wen: Tzu. Shanghai: Crescent Moon Press, 1930.
The Correspondence of a Genius. Shanghai: Ta-kuang Press, 1936.
The Diary of a Stupid Officer. Shanghai: Far Eastern Press, 1929.
The Diary of a Woman. Shanghai: Kuo-hua Press, 1937.
The Diary of the Non-dead. Shanghai: Human World Press, 1929.
The Ducks. Peking: Pei-hsin Press, 1926.
The Eight Steeds. Shanghai: Cultural Life Press, 1935; Hong Kong: Jih-hsin Book Company, 1960.
The Fourteenth Night. Place unknown: Press unknown, 1928.
An Honest Man. Place unknown: Press unknown, 1928.
The Housewife. Kunming: Commercial Press, 1939.
The Inn and Others. Shanghai: Chung-hua Press, 1930.
In the Army. Shanghai: Pei-hsin Press, 1928.
Ju-jui Chi. Shanghai: Cultural Life Press, 1934.
The Life of an Actress. Shanghai: Ta-t'ung Press, 1931.
Long River. Hong Kong: Wen-li Press, 1960.
Mandarin Oranges. Peking: Crescent Moon Press, 1927.
A Meddlesome Person. Shanghai: Crescent Moon Press, 1928.
A Mother. Shanghai: Ho-cheng Book Store, 1933.
The New and the Old. Kunming: Liang-yu Press, 1943.
Pebble Ferry. Shanghai: Chung-hua Press, 1931.
Scenes Under the Moon. Hong Kong: Wen-li Press, 1960.

The Selected Stories and Essays of Shen Ts'ung-wen. Hong Kong:
New Learning Press, 1957.
Selected Stories of Ts'ung-wen. Shanghai: Ta-kuang Press, 1936.
Selected Works of Ts'ung-wen. Shanghai: Wan-hsiang Press, 1936;
Hong Kong: Literature Press, 1956.
The Selected Works of Shen Ts'ung-wen. Peking: People's Literature
Press, 1957.
Sinking. Place unknown: Press unknown, 1930.
Spring. Hong Kong: Wen-li Press, 1960.
Spring and Lamp. Hong Kong: Wen-li Press, 1960.
Tiger Cub. Shanghai: New China Press, 1932.
What Men Should Know. Shanghai: Red and Black Press, 1929.
The Witch Doctor's Love. Hong Kong: Wen-li Press, 1960.

2. Nonfiction

Autobiography of Ts'ung-wen. Hong Kong: Wen-li Press, 1960.
Bronze Mirrors in the T'ang and Sung Dynasties. Peking: Chinese
Classical Art Press, 1958.
Designs in Chinese Silk and Linen. Peking: Chinese Classical Art
Press, 1957.
In Reminiscence of Hu Yeh-p'in. Shanghai: Kuang-hua Press, 1932.
In Reminiscence of Ting Ling. Shanghai: Liang-yu Press, 1934.
In Reminiscence of Ting Ling, Continued. Shanghai: Liang-yu Press,
1939.
Letters Saved from Oblivion. Kunming: K'ai-ming Press, 1943.
Random Sketches on a Trip to West Hunan. Kunming: K'ai-ming
Press, 1943.
Watching Clouds in Yünnan. Chungking: National Readers' Press,
1943.
West Hunan. Kunming: K'ai-ming Press, 1944.
Winter Scenes in Kunming. Kunming: Cultural Life Press, 1939.

3. Miscellaneous Writings

Chiao-hsiu and Tung-sheng. Peking: *Literary Magazine,* 1947. II.
Festivals and Lanterns. Peking: *People's Literature,* 1963.
How Should We Read New Poetry? (Place unknown): *An Anthol-
ogy of Criticisms on Modern Poetry,* 1934.
Maid Wang, in *Five Years of Fiction Writing.* Chungking: Chien-kuo
Press, 1932. I-III.
Morning on the Ching-kang Mountain. Peking: *People's Literature,*
1962.

My Learning. Hong Kong: Ta-kung Pao, November 19-22, 1951. pp. unknown.

On Modern Chinese Fiction, in *An Anthology of Modern Chinese Fiction.* Feng-t'ien: Orient Press, 1935.

The Red Incubus. Peking: *Literary Magazine,* 1947. II.

A Romance Quite Ordinary. Peking: *Literary Magazine,* 1947. II.

Some Memories, Some Thoughts. Peking: *People's Literature,* 1957. Volume unknown.

Some Thoughts on Modern Chinese Literature, in *Chinese Literature Reader,* I. Shanghai: Ts'un Chung Press, 1931.

Speech Given by Shen Ts'ung-wen. Peking: *Kuang-ming Jih-pao,* February 8, 1956.

Story Untitled, in *An Anthology of Modern Chinese Fiction.* Feng-t'ien: Orient Press, 1935.

Sunshine After Snow. Peking: *Literary Magazine,* 1947. II.

A Supporting Role. Peking: *People's Literature,* July, 1957. Volume unknown.

White Nightmare, in *Anthology of Stories from the War.* Place, Press, Date unknown.

SECONDARY SOURCES

This list includes selected articles, critical essays, and histories of modern Chinese literature; asterisks indicate Chinese language sources.

*CHAO TS'UNG. *Random Talks on the May Fourth Movement.* Hong Kong: Union Press, 1964.

*CH'EN TU-HSIU. *Collected Works of Tu-hsiu.* Shanghai: Ya-tung Book Co. 1922.

CHOW TSE-TSUNG. *Research Guide to the May Fourth Movement.* Cambridge: Harvard University Press, 1963.

————. *The May Fourth Movement: Intellectual Revolution in Modern China.* Cambridge: Harvard University Press, 1960.

*CHU KUANG-CH'IEN. *Modern Chinese Literature.* Peking: *Literary Magazine,* 1947. II.

*HAN SHIH-HENG. *Mr. Shen Ts'ung-wen's Fiction,* in *Selected Essays of Literary Criticism.* Shanghai: Modern Press, 1934.

HO KAN-CHIH. *A History of the Modern Chinese Revolution.* Peking: Foreign Language Press, 1959.

*HO YÜ-PO. *Criticisms on Modern Chinese Writers.* Shanghai: Kuang-hua Press, 1932.

HSIA, C. T. *A History of Modern Chinese Fiction.* New Haven: Yale University Press, 1961.

HUANG SUNG-KANG. *Lu Hsün and the New Culture Movement of Modern China*. Amsterdam: Djambatan, 1957.

*KU FENG-CH'ENG. *Introduction to a New Literature*. Shanghai: Kuanghua Press, 1930.

*LIANG, SHIH-CH'IU. *Random Talks on Hsu Chih-mo*. Taipei: Far Eastern Press, 1958.

*LIU HSI-WEI. "On *The Border Town*, and *Eight Steeds*." Peking: *Literary Quarterly*, 1935. II.

*MA FENG-HUA. "In Reminiscence of Professor Shen Ts'ung-wen." Taipei: *Biographical Literature*, 1957. II.

MENDE, TIBOR. *The Chinese Revolution*. London: Thames and Hudson, 1961.

PRIESTLY, K. E. *China's Men of Letters*. Hong Kong: Dragonfly Books, 1962.

TENG SSU-YU, and FAIRBANK, J. K. *China's Response to the West: A Documentary Survey 1839-1923*. Cambridge: Harvard University Press, 1966.

*TING LING. *The Life of an Honest Man*, preface to *Selected Works of Hu Yeh-p'in*. Shanghai: K'ai-ming Press, 1951.

TING YI. *A Short History of Modern Chinese Literature*. Peking: Foreign Language Press, 1959.

TREGEAR, T. R. *A Geography of China*. Chicago: Aldine Publishing Co., 1965.

*TS'AO CHÜ-JEN. *Fifty Years of the Chinese Literary Scene*. Hong Kong: New Culture Press, 1969.

*TU LING. *About Shen Ts'ung-wen*. Hong Kong: *Hot Wind*, May 1956. Nos. 56-57.

*WANG CHE-FU. *A History of the New Chinese Literary Movement*. Hong Kong: Far Eastern Press, 1965.

*WANG YAO. *A Draft History of Modern Chinese Literature*. Shanghai: New Literature Press, 1953.

Translations into English of Shen Ts'ung-wen's work.

CHING TI and PAYNE, ROBERT. *The Chinese Earth*. London: George Allen and Unwin, Ltd., 1947.

LEE YI-HSIEH. *Hsiao-hsiao*, in *Tien Hsia Monthly*. Place unknown, October, 1938. III, 3.

Index